AMAZING

BLUNDERS
AND
BUNGLES

Including
AMAZING BLUNDERS AND BUNGLES
AMAZING HOAXES AND FRAUDS

PETER ELDIN

DEAN

in association with Hamlyn Children's Books

Published in 1992 by
Dean, part of Reed International Books Ltd.,
Michelin House, 81 Fulham Road, London SW3 6RB
Text by Peter Eldin, Data Forum Ltd.
Illustrated by Kim Blundell
Cover by Mik Brown

This material first appeared under the titles:
Amazing Hoaxes and Frauds
Amazing Blunders and Bungles

ISBN 0603550207

Printed in Great Britain by The Bath Press

AMAZING

BLUNDERS
AND
BUNGLES

Introduction

Did you ever hear of the prisoners who tunnelled out of their cell – straight into a courtroom? Or the bride who got married – to the best man? Would you believe that an army of policemen spent a day trying to lift a 'stolen safe' – only to discover that it was an electricity junction box?

Well, nobody's perfect! We humans can make the most hilarious mistakes and miscalculations, and this book is full of them: botched robberies, devastating clerical errors, newspaper misprints, political boobs, actors' 'fluffs', and unbelievable slip-ups.

If you don't believe just how *silly* people can be – read on!

Free Flight

The plane-load of passengers flying from Manchester to London with British Airways got a bargain flight. The cabin crew on the walk-on shuttle service forgot to collect the fares. By the time they realized their mistake the 130 passengers had left Heathrow and British Airways had lost £5265 in fares!

I've Lost My Wife

On 24 March, 1978, Harry Allison was sitting in his office at the Southwaite services area on the M6 motorway in England when a man burst in crying, 'I've lost my wife!'

Apparently the man had got out of his car at a previous service area. When he returned he assumed that his wife was still asleep on the back seat. He never thought to look and he drove 40 miles before he discovered that she, too, had left the car.

Another Charioteer

In the film, *Ben Hur*, which takes place in ancient Rome, there is a magnificent chariot race. But the director boobed slightly, for in the scene, a red sports car can be seen passing by in the distance.

Winning Mistake

Tony Jarvis went to Thirsk races in northern England to watch the horse he had selected as a potential winner. Without realizing it, he had mistakenly put a bet on a horse in the 3.15 race instead of the 2.45 race as he had intended. That mistake made him a lot of money; instead of winning only a few pounds, he ended up with £28 281!

8

Cruel Cut

When people complained about the over-grown garden in Akron, Ohio, USA, the council sent some of their men to cut down the weeds. It proved to be an expensive exercise as a judge later ordered the council to pay £1000 compensation to the householder. He was a vegetarian and had been growing weeds to eat.

Hold-up Slip-up

Would-be bank robber, Carlo Colondi, really slipped up when he tried to rob a bank in Milan, Italy. As he burst through the door he tripped on the doormat, his scarf fell from his face and his gun went off harmlessly.

He got up and headed for the cashier — only to slip over again on the floor.

Confused by the customers and staff laughing at him, Colondi rushed out to his car — only to be arrested; he'd left his car in a no-parking area.

Hotel Hanky Panky

The manager of the Waldorf-Astoria Hotel in New York had quite a job pacifying several guests who had been woken early by mistake. He faced even more problems when people who should have been called early came down later to complain that they had not been called.

And then he was bombarded by complaints from guests who were trying to telephone out of the hotel but could not do so because all the lines were blocked.

The reason for all the problems eventually became clear. It was the first day they had tried their new computerized telephone system, which was having 'teething troubles'.

Armed Robber

An armed masked man raided a bank in Kentucky, USA, and may have got away with it but for one thing. It was a hot day, so he had rolled up his sleeves, forgetting he had a tattoo on his arm — with his name on it!

Young Driver

The computer at the Driver and Vehicle Licensing Centre in Swansea, Wales, once sent out a reminder to a young lady that her driving licence was due to be renewed. The lady did not take any notice of the reminder, but it was hardly surprising. She was, after all, only six years old!

Ward Discovery

Builders working on an extension to a hospital in Mozambique, south-east Africa, uncovered a gigantic blunder when they knocked a hole through a wall. On the other side they found a fully-equipped maternity ward containing some £50 000 worth of equipment. Someone had apparently walled up the ward by accident and hospital authorities had forgotten it was there!

11

Navy Parade

American Secretary of State, William Jennings, invited the Swiss Navy to attend the grand opening of the Panama Canal. The Swiss, in case you didn't know, don't have a navy as they do not have a coast!

What a Gas!

From 1970 to 1972 Mrs Claire Bamber of Blackburn, England tried to convince gas officials that she had no gas meter in her all-electric home. But the Gas Board computer said that there was a meter there, so gas-men continued to call at her house to read it. She received cards asking her to fill in the figures from the non-existent meter so a bill could be sent to her.

Mrs Bamber got so fed up with this, she put a set of ridiculous figures on a card and sent it off. The Gas Board sent an inspector to the house to see what was going on and Mrs Bamber explained she had no gas meter. The inspector apologized and promised that she would not be bothered again. Then another meter card arrived!

On the day the gas-man was due to call, she went to work leaving a note pinned to her front door: 'Confession is good for the soul. I'm getting free gas'. When she got home she was met by several gas-men and policemen!

Once again she had to explain that she did not use gas – and this time the gas officials made sure that the computer got the message.

Gone to Launch

eport of a boat launch that appeared in a magazine:

'. . . the Admiral's lovely daughter smashed a bottle of champagne over her stern as she slid gracefully down the slipway.'

Disaster Drive

W hen Eric Green and his family set off to Eric's brother's wedding in April, 1985, they allowed plenty of time for the journey of 160 miles. They were up at the crack of dawn and left the house at 6.45am. They did not have to be at the wedding until 3pm.

They were only 3 miles from home when the oil light flashed on their Granada's dashboard — the oil pump had stopped working. As they had not gone very far they decided to drive slowly back home. They then borrowed a friend's Mercedes and the three of them set off again. They still had plenty of time for the journey. Five miles down the road they heard a bang beneath the car — the centre bearing of the prop shaft had partially collapsed! Once again the Greens headed back for home.

14

Next they borrowed a Jaguar from another friend. Everything was fine until they had reached about half way. Then came a knocking from the engine. It was a faulty piston!

As they still had plenty of time, they decided to go back home once again and fetch Mrs Green's Alfa Romeo. They got home at 12.15pm – only to find that the car had been stolen!

This time they borrowed a Vauxhall Victor from Mr Green's sister. The car was old but they thought that nothing else could possibly go wrong. But it did – a tyre burst!

When they had had a new tyre fitted they continued their journey without further mishap. They arrived well after the wedding – at 5.30pm. It had taken nearly 11 hours to make the journey.

Late on Parade

In 1985, Juanita Johnson was driving through March in Cambridgeshire, England, when she was stopped by the mayor and mayoress who were in full regalia. They explained that they should have been present at the gala celebrations and asked Juanita to catch up with the floats parading through the town. This she did then, with the mayor and mayoress standing with their heads out of her sun roof, she drove along at the head of the procession.

Mayor George Brewin was rather embarrassed by the situation. So were the gala organizers when the mayor asked why the official car had not turned up on time. It had been decided not to ask the mayor and mayoress to lead the 1985 parade, but no one had informed the mayor of that decision!

Missed!

During the Peruvian Air Force Week in 1975, 30 fighter planes took part in a demonstration of their prowess. Fourteen old fishing boats were towed out to sea and the Peruvian air force flew in for the attack. For the next 15 minutes the target vessels were bombed and strafed to the delight of the watching crowd. But at the end of the display, the admiration of the onlookers turned to amazement. Not one of the 14 vessels had been hit!

Train Trap

A burglar was just about to leave a department store in Hamburg, West Germany when he spotted a model train set. He was still playing with it three hours later when the police arrived!

Ploughman's Crunch

Farmer, Anton Barton, got so hot while ploughing his field in South Carolina, USA, that he stopped for a refreshing drink of beer. It was so tasty, he continued drinking during the rest of the day. After work he set off to his home. Unfortunately, all that beer had made him rather tipsy and he forgot to raise the plough. By the time police caught up with him he had ploughed up 2 miles of roadway!

Slippery Customer

When the thief in Sheffield, England, saw an upstairs window of a house slightly open, he thought he was on to a good thing. He shinned up the drainpipe and let himself in. The room was occupied by a 4-metre (13-foot) boa constrictor. The thief quickly backed out of the window, forgetting he was upstairs, and ended up with a broken leg.

Ambulancemen Anglers

Two hundred ambulancemen lined up along the banks of a canal in Kidderminster, England, to take part in the annual angling championship. After five hours, no one had caught a fish. Someone had forgotten to tell the organizer that the fish had been removed to another location three weeks earlier.

Grave Mistake

The funeral of 56-year-old Antonio Percelli at Palermo in Sicily went according to plan – until he climbed out of his coffin. But the efforts of the funeral directors were not wasted. The shock of Antonio stepping out of his grave caused his mother-in-law to have a heart attack. She was buried in the grave instead of him.

The Last Supper?

During the month of May, Henekey's steak bar will be supporting the Mayor's appeal for £45 000 towards an Emisonic Scanner for Windsor's King Edward VII Hospital.

For every customer who dies in the bar during the month, 20p will be donated towards the fund.

(Staines Informer)

Royal Faux Pas

The novelist, John Buchan, was proud to be presented to King George V in 1935. He was even prouder when, during their conversation, the King mentioned how much he enjoyed Buchan's books, especially *The Thirty Nine Steps*. Later that day Queen Mary was talking to the novelist. She said, 'The King does not get much time for reading, but when he does he reads the most awful rubbish.'

Street Scene

During a performance of Mozart's opera, *Don Giovanni*, at the City Center, New York, USA, the audience were amazed when they suddenly saw a modern street scene before them. By mistake all the scenery used in the production had been raised at the same time that the outer doors at the back of the stage were opened. Instead of 18th-century Spain, the audience saw 20th-century New York!

On Reflection

Many blunders are made in film-making and a lot of mistakes actually appear on the finished film. One of the most obvious appeared in the 1954 film, *Carmen Jones*. In one shot the camera follows the heroine along a street but the film-makers did not notice, until the film was released, that a reflection of the camera was visible in every shop window.

We're (Not) Getting There

An advertising slogan used by British Rail is 'We're getting there'. But Sir Peter Parker, Chairman of British Rail took a long time to get 'there' in July, 1979.

He had planned to travel by train to a meeting with Cumbria County Council. Unfortunately he was delayed by traffic and he arrived at Crewe station just as his train was drawing out. He ran through the ticket barrier and scrambled on to the train.

Once he had settled down for the journey Sir Peter realized that he was on the wrong train. Instead of heading towards Carlisle it was travelling south, non-stop to London! When he arrived in the capital the chairman of British Rail headed again for Cumbria. But this time he took no chances — he travelled by aeroplane!

Crash, Bang, Wallop

Romark was a successful hypnotist and mind-reader and had his own series on British television. On 12th October, 1977, he prepared to perform one of the amazing psychic feats for which he had become famous. Two coins were placed over his eyes. These were covered with dough which was held in place by thick bandages tied around his head. It was impossible for him to see anything but Romark was confident that his incredible powers would enable him to drive a car through the streets of Ilford, Essex, whilst blindfolded. He got into the yellow Renault and proceeded down Cranbrook Road. Seconds later his confidence and his reputation were shattered. He crashed straight into the back of a stationary police car!

Pocketful of Trouble

During a game of pool in a bar in North London, one of the players made a 'foul' shot by hitting the white ball into a pocket.

It should have rolled along a track and been returned at the end of the table, but it got stuck and did not come back. As the game could not continue without the ball, the barmaid, Lynn McAnally, offered to help by putting her hand into the pocket to see if she could release the ball. It was no use, and when Lynn tried to remove her arm, she found she was stuck. Her arm was trapped up to the elbow.

They tried pouring oil, and even ice, down the machine but Lynn remained trapped. Someone tried operating the ball release mechanism but this only resulted in pinching the girl's fingers.

Lynn had to remain trapped in the pool table for an hour and a half until firemen eventually released her by pulling the table to pieces.

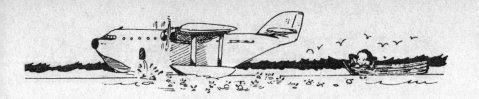

Crying Tonight

Chris's Fish Bar in Grays, Essex, England, had £500 wrapped up ready for banking on 11 August, 1986. But the money disappeared. One of the staff wrapped it up instead of a portion of chips, and gave it to a customer!

Say 'Cheese'

The two thieves charged with raiding a golf club were surprised when police offered them each a piece of cheese. It was to lead to their downfall for their toothmarks exactly matched those found in a piece of cheese left in the golf clubhouse.

25

Mammoth Mistake

In Eastbourne, England, it was decided that Father Christmas would ride on a sledge pulled by an elephant as part of the 1986 Christmas parade. But Lola, the elephant, did not think much of the idea.

She dumped Father Christmas in a flower bed in front of surprised onlookers. The sledge smashed into parked cars and the elephant lumbered up the steps of the Cavendish Court Hotel by herself.

Tasty Deal

Rover 3500. Fitted sun roof, radio, heated rear window. Also fresh farm eggs, vegetables, exhaust, tyres, seals, front wings, exchange differential.

(Maidenhead Advertiser)

Tramp's Ball

Nancy Reagan, wife of the American President Ronald Reagan, thought she had planned everything down to the finest detail for the Queen of England's visit to the White House in 1980. But she blundered on one important point – the music for the Queen's dance with the President. As the Queen and the President moved on to the dance floor, the band played *The Lady is a Tramp*.

All At Sea

The cleaners on a British cross-channel ferry had quite a shock when they finished their work one day in September, 1985. They went up on deck to find that they were on their way to France. They had been so busy at their work they had not noticed the ship leave harbour. The twelve women and one man had to transfer to a Navy pilot launch to get home.

Doggone!

Mia Wood tied her alsatian, Tara, to a stall outside a fruit shop in Tranent, Scotland, while she went in to do some shopping. A few seconds later she heard a terrific crash outside the shop. When she went to investigate she was horrified to see Tara running off down the road, still attached to the fruit stall! Shoppers had to leap for their lives as the dog and the stall careered down Fleets Road with fruit and vegetables flying in all directions. Luckily, no real harm was done.

Floating Theatre

On 13 February, 1979, architects met on Skegness Pier on the north-east coast of England to present George Sunderland with an award for the best-designed pier theatre.

During the presentation ceremony, the theatre was swept out to sea.

Hat Trick

A gunman who robbed a Paris grocer thought he had got away scot-free. But as he ran away, his hat blew off. It was not long before the police caught up with him – his name and address were inside the hat.

The Mayor's Mistake

T he firemen in the Swiss town of Corcelles-Cormondrec had not been called out to a fire for 20 years. The mayor felt they must be getting bored with this inactivity so he organized a day trip for them. It proved to be a costly mistake. While they were out enjoying themselves, the mayor's office caught fire!

Fish Dip

Angler, Danny Cullen, decided to use his car headlights to attract a pike he was trying to catch. Unfortunately, he drove too near to the edge of the flooded gravel pit at Rickmansworth, Hertfordshire in England and his car sank into the water.

Man Who Dropped a Gold Brick

Everyone makes mistakes, but in 1880, George Harrison, a gold prospector in South Africa made a very expensive one when he sold his claim in the Witwatersrand goldfield for £10. He had found gold on the site but had no real faith in the possibility of finding any more.

Over the next year, the claim changed hands three more times; the third time for £2000 plus £8000 in shares. It continued to gain in value and became the centre of the entire South African gold-mining industry.

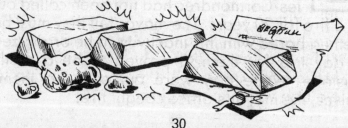

Digger Dog

An Australian tennis club made a big mistake when it employed an alsatian dog to guard the courts before an important tournament. During the night, the dog dug up 8 square metres (9 square yards) of the centre court. He was looking for bones!

Be Prepared

A bank robber went up to the cashier of a bank in Oregon, USA, and pushed a note across the counter. It read: 'This is a hold-up and I've got a gun. Put all the money in a paper bag.'

The cashier read the note and then wrote on it, 'I don't have a paper bag.' The confused robber fled as quickly as he could, probably vowing to take a bag with him next time.

Opera Hang-Up

In 1956, the opera singer, Hans Hotter, strode on to the stage of the Royal Opera House, London, during Act Three of *Die Walküre.* He was greeted by roars of laughter. He had been in such a rush to put on his cloak, he had not noticed the coat hanger sticking out of his collar!

Repeat Showing

On 31 December, 1986, millions of West Germans sat down to watch their President's New Year speech on television. When Herr von Weizsaecker began talking, many viewers thought that the speech had a familiar ring to it. Those with good memories soon realized that the President was saying exactly the same as he had the year before.

Later that evening, television chiefs of State Channel 2DF apologized for the fact that engineers had put on the previous year's taped speech by mistake.

Head Start

As a jumbo jet was taxiing towards its take-off runway at Heathrow Airport one day in December, 1986, one of the passengers decided to open his overhead locker. A bottle of whisky fell out and landed on the head of another passenger. The jet had to turn back so a nurse could be brought on board, and the plane was delayed for two hours.

Where's the Match?

In 1983, 50 fans of the Scottish football team, Celtic, travelled to Germany to watch their team play in Nuremburg. After 1000 miles of travel, they eagerly pushed their way through the stadium turnstiles and went into an athletics meeting! Celtic were playing against Nuremburg — but 200 miles away in Konstanz!

On the Tiles

Ray Strank was pleased with the roof tiling he finished on 27 November, 1984. He had spent two days on the job in Wimbledon, London, and was very happy with the result. But his boss, brother Gordon, was furious when he saw it. Ray had tiled the wrong house!

The lady in the house, who had been supplying tea for Ray whilst the work was being done, was just as embarrassed as he was. She had assumed that her husband had ordered the work to be done!

Design Fault

A new factory at Warrington in England had been voted a design award for excellence. The Royal Institute of British Architects was to make a special presentation of the award. However, the judges changed their minds when part of the roof collapsed!

Car Climber

W hen American scientists tested their new, driverless car in 1985, things did not go exactly as planned. The six-wheeled vehicle, called the Terregator, was designed to use computerized cameras to scan the road ahead and then automatically go in the correct direction. Unfortunately, there had been some miscalculation by the scientists of the Robotics Institute in Pittsburgh.

The vehicle was tested along a wooden path. All went well until the bends became a little sharper. The car veered off the track and ended up by trying to climb up a tree!

State Secret?

A REMITTANCE PRINCE? While the British press speculates that Prince Andrew is being sent to Lakefield College School to help Canada through a constitutional crisis, our sources tell us the real reaxon for the prince's being sent to Cannadda in midterm is that heb xng bi& ng 8! ((prondi iic456 – % BNOThb;t cppty whhhhhhenn e9090 () () whch isssn't too sprising to those who know the boy's private interests.

(*Toronto Sun*)

Thief Who Talked Too Much

D uring a burglary in 1980, robber, John Yianni, narrowly escaped being caught. Afterwards, he telephoned his flat where a friend was waiting to hear from him, and described what had happened. 'Why don't you come round and tell me about it?' said his friend. Yianni went to the flat and was promptly arrested. It was not his friend to whom he had been talking. It was a policeman.

Fire Hazard

Someone slipped up in Clairton, Pennsylvania USA when it was decided to buy a sleek 13-metre- (43-foot)-long fire engine for the town. It was so long it could not be used on most of the town's narrow streets. Embarrassed town officials had to return the new fire engine and exchange it for two smaller models.

Named In Error

In the early 1950s a woman was asked to launch a yacht in Bermuda. Twice she tried to break a bottle of champagne against its bows but both times she failed. The boat slid down the slipway as the woman cried, 'Oh, I can't.'

The yacht was therefore named *Oh I Cant*!

Marathon Madness

A family in Manchester decided, one Sunday, to go out for lunch. But as they drove into Manchester they got boxed in by official cars in a marathon race. There was absolutely no way out and they ended up having to drive the complete 26-mile marathon course before they could finally escape to a late lunch!

Swallow That!

Bob Arneill had not visited a dentist for 15 years, but a painful tooth eventually forced him to go in 1985. It was not long before he wished he had not bothered. The dentist looked into his mouth and accidentally dropped a 4-centimetre (1½-inch) -long dental instrument into Bob's mouth. Unfortunately Bob swallowed it and had to be rushed to hospital.

Pulling the Plug

Workers clearing rubbish from the Chester-field-Stockwith Canal in England, in 1978, were very surprised when all the water suddenly vanished. What they had not realized was that one of the old bits of metal they had removed was a 200-year-old plug that ensured the existence of the canal. When it was removed, all the water ran into the hole – leaving several angry boat people high and dry!

Crumbs!

Chris Brown, managing director of Brown's Bakery in Nottingham, England, was very pleased when he heard about the order for 200 dozen (2400) rolls. Employees worked through the night to meet the order, but on the next day, 12 December, 1986, it was discovered that a shop assistant had bungled the order. She had written 200 dozen rolls but the order was really for just 200. The bakery had made 2200 rolls too many!

Too much of a Good Thing

A crook once thought that he had planned the perfect crime. He hid in a shop until it had closed and then crept out to begin loading goods into two suitcases he had with him. But when he found some brandy, he decided to try a drop, and then a drop more and then a little drop more.

Next morning he realized that his crime had not been a success. He had drunk too much brandy the night before and had fallen asleep. When he awoke he discovered that he was lying in the shop's window and that he was being stared at by quite a crowd of passers-by!

Wardrobe Distress Signal

A Russian satellite picked up a distress signal from what was believed to be a ship in distress. Operators at a ground terminal in Toulouse, France, picked up the signal and pin-pointed the vessel to be in the Firth of Clyde area of Scotland. The French authorities notified the British, and a Royal Air Force helicopter was sent out on a mercy mission. Vessels in the Clyde estuary were also asked to begin a thorough search for the vessel.

After six hours of searching, the helicopter located the source of the signal – a council house at Pitreavie in Fife. The RAF pilot and a policeman were sent to investigate, and found that the signal was coming from an old distress beacon dumped on top of a wardrobe!

Flower Food

A nd when they turn brown with age, they can be cut and dried to make one of the increasingly popular fried flower arrangements.
(*Rhymney Valley Express*)

Love Link

When Jane Totty of Birmingham, England, left her hotel job in October, 1986, her friends arranged a party for her and employed Steve McAllister to dress up as a policeman. He put a pair of handcuffs on her for a joke but when he tried to take them off again, he could not find the key. The real police were called but they could not free poor Jane either. Eventually the fire brigade was called and they had to hack the cuffs off!

In The News

Farmer, Christos Kalimeris, made the mistake of buying all the newspapers from the only kiosk in his village of Psathopygo, near Patras, Greece. His fellow villagers were up in arms because they could not read the latest news. A lawyer on holiday in the area had Kalimeris arrested for 'restricting access to information'. The farmer had not intended to upset anyone. He just wanted the papers to line his pig sties to keep his new-born piglets warm!

Automatic Chaos

John Rimmer has cause to remember the day in 1985, when he first drove a car with an automatic clutch. He stopped for petrol in Liverpool, England. The petrol attendant asked for the car to be moved back slightly and then the trouble began. John got his foot stuck between the accelerator and the brake pedal and the Metro shot backwards. A petrol-pump hose was caught and the pump was pulled over. The car door was open and caught the garage attendant, carrying him 18 metres (20 yards) across the forecourt. If that was not enough damage for one day, the car then sped out into the road and crashed into a parked car!

The petrol station had to be closed down for the day, the attendant had to go into hospital and John Rimmer was fined £25 and had his licence endorsed for careless driving. He also lost his job – as a driving instructor.

Lucky Bet

A man from Warwickshire, England, used to bet on horse races every Saturday. One day, he was unable to get to the betting-shop himself so he asked his wife to place his bets for him. She arrived at the betting shop but could remember only three of the four horses her husband had selected. For the fourth horse she backed a horse with a name that appealed to her.

When she told her husband, he was furious — until he checked the results later that day. His wife's mistake had won them £2250!

What A Corker

P hilip Barret, a watchmaker, was alarmed when a masked man came into his shop, pointed a gun at him and said, 'This is a stick up!'

But Mr Barret was not alarmed for very long, for the raider had made one vital blunder — he had left the cork in the pop-gun he was using.

44

High Flyer

I t seemed a good idea to Larry Walters — tie some gas balloons to a deck-chair and then take off. He tied 42 gas-filled balloons to the chair and the system worked better than he had expected. Within minutes, he was flying 3 miles high — and still climbing. It gave pilots from the nearby Long Beach Airport, near Los Angeles, USA, quite a shock. They reported a strange man flying in a deck chair.

Larry was eventually able to land after bursting some of the balloons with his pen-knife. But when he landed he was immediately charged for flying without a licence!

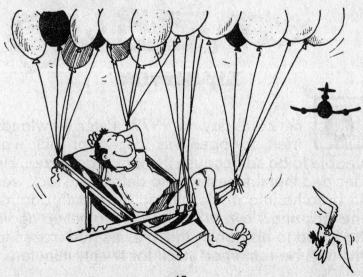

45

Mountain Muck-up

To mark the 40th anniversary of the United Nations in 1985 it was decided to ask climbers to scale Mount Everest and plant a UN flag on the summit. But the expedition ended in a blunder. Unfortunately for the climbers, they picked a time when the weather was the worst it had been for many years. Although they managed to brave the cold and the incessant winds they were forced to abandon the climb 240 metres (800 feet) from the summit. Even that is quite a remarkable achievement — but the climbers slipped up when they planted the flag and took a photograph. The flag was upside down!

Lip Service

One cold day in 1979, Peter Rowlands tried to open his car door but was unable to do so because the lock was frozen. He decided that the best way to defrost the lock was to breathe into it. He placed his mouth against the lock and blew. When he went to get up again he found to his horror that his lips had frozen to the car! He remained stuck for twenty minutes.

46

Red Over Heels

Russians had a good laugh early in 1985 when some new boots reached the shops. They all had heels attached to the toe end of the foot!

Gospel Music

Catholic nuns of the Mission of Jesus, Mary and Joseph, with a television success behind them and Mother Superior Francisca at the guitar, are bidding here for fame and fortune in the pope charts.

(Evening Post)

What a Dud

Armed bandits ambushed a bank van in London on 24 April, 1985. They stole eight bags of cheques, dumped them into two waiting cars and drove off. They intended to cash the cheques made out for large amounts, but they must have received quite a shock when they opened the bags. All the cheques had already been cancelled and were therefore useless to them.

Up In The Air

It had been decided to remove the 18-metre (60-foot)-high elm tree near Hurstbourne Tarrant, Hampshire in England because of the danger of it falling on a nearby barn. Therefore on 22 March, 1985, a team of woodcutters wrapped a chain around the tree and fixed the other end to a winch on a tractor. The winch was switched on and the men stood back waiting for the tree to topple. But the tree was not so near to falling down as everyone had thought. It would not budge. Instead the tractor was hauled up the tree!

The red-faced woodcutters had to get a crane to rescue the tractor!

Who's Baby

Political parties are usually very careful about the things they put into their literature. Every care was taken with a pamphlet prepared by the Labour Party in 1948. On the front was a photograph of a baby who was 'growing up healthily under a Labour government' led by Prime Minister Clement Attlee. The pamphlet was published as planned – but it had to be withdrawn rather hastily when someone recognized the baby on the front cover. It was the infant Duke of Kent!

Fire!

Caroline McKenna was working in the Ship Inn, Wokingham, in southern England, when two firemen rushed in and asked to use the telephone. They called the fire brigade to come out urgently – their fire-engine was on fire!

Escape to Prison

In June, 1982, Thomas Gee had completed only two months of his 12-month prison sentence. He did not fancy the idea of another ten months behind bars, so he was determined to escape. He was working in the prison's vegetable store when he saw his chance. A lorry arrived with a delivery of vegetables and Thomas quickly dashed underneath it and held on to part of the chassis.

When he had completed his delivery at the prison, the driver set off to his next stop, little knowing that he was carrying a passenger. Thomas clung to the chassis for some time until the lorry eventually slowed down and stopped. Covered in oil, he slipped from his hiding place – and was met by two prison officers. The lorry's second delivery was at another jail – Thomas had escaped from one prison to another!

You are Discharged

A Royal Air Force airman was surprised to receive notice that he was to be discharged from the service. He was even more surprised when he read the reason – he was pregnant! The computer had made an error.

Silly Sausage

T he *Staines and Egham News*, an English local paper, once reported that 'Mr George Dobbs, of Chertsey, is very proud of the fact that he walked 50 miles on a sausage sandwich at the weekend.'

Coup De Grass

The Ladies Circle of West End Esher in Surrey, England were pleased with all the goods they had collected for their jumble sale, early in 1985. One of the items was a lawn mower. They sold the mower for £20 but then discovered that the mower belonged to the local cricket club and it was worth £300.

No one knew the man who had bought the mower but one woman remembered that he had a beard and he mentioned the fact that he often visited jumble sales in the area. So the ladies sent their members to all the jumble sales within a radius of 15 miles. Their plan worked and they found the bearded man. Unfortunately, he had already resold the mower to a man who had not given either his name or address.

Where There's a Will, There's a Way

GREENWOLD, Florence May. — Late of 163 Bergholt Road, Colchester. A simple, kind, and loving old lady who died with great dignity at 'Ambleside', Wood Lane, Fordham Heath, Colchester on Saturday, April 3, 1982 at 3.10pm. Loved by family and friends who knew her will.

(*Essex County Standard*)

Victorian Television

The film, *The Wrong Box*, is an amusing comedy set in Victorian times, the end of the 19th century. But one of the jokes was completely unintentional. The film-makers allowed television aerials on the rooftops to be seen in the film, forgetting that television was not invented until 1926!

What's My Name?

Broadcasters quite often get their lines wrong, but Bill Hardcastle once got his own name wrong. He finished a news bulletin on Northern Ireland by saying: 'This is The World at One with William Whitelaw.' (William Whitelaw was then the Home Secretary!)

Medal Winner

When Francisco Ayala retired from the Spanish state railways in 1977 he was presented with a gold medal to mark his 50 years' service. When he examined the medal he found that it was only gold plated. The plated medal was worth about £25 whereas the real thing would have been worth over £300. Ayala took the railway company to court. The judge ruled that 'any man who works for one company for 50 years deserves a real gold medal.'

The railway company had no alternative but to give Francisco a real gold medal, whereupon they were faced with over 60 more claims from retired workers!

Lock Up Before You Go

Three bandits who held up a bank in La Jara, Colorado, USA, proved quite successful. When they had collected enough money, they shut the bank staff in a strongroom, thinking that would give them time to get away. But they made one vital mistake — they forgot to lock the strongroom. The bank staff were able to walk out of the strongroom and raise the alarm, and the burglars were soon caught.

Witch Report

A Nigerian woman threatened to put a voodoo on her after a row. The woman herself was not available last night. A neighbour said she had gone away for a short spell.

(Daily Express)

Flight Delay

Computers are such an important part of everyday life that we tend to take them for granted. Many people believe that computers cannot make a mistake. But they can go wrong and, when they do, the result is often absolute chaos. This was certainly the case on 6 October, 1986, when there was a fault in an air traffic control computer at Heathrow Airport, causing considerable congestion of both aeroplanes and people.

It took two hours to repair the fault. Many of the outgoing flights had to be cancelled and incoming flights had to be delayed by up to six hours.

Air Mail

I t is not very often that a letter-box is positioned nearly 3 metres (9 feet) above the ground. But it happened in Ballymacra, County Antrim, Ireland in March, 1979.

The telegraph pole to which the letter-box had been fixed had had to be replaced. But there were no keys available to release the bands holding the letter-box in place so it was slid off the top off the pole. When the replacement pole was in position, the letter-box was slid back over it. Unfortunately, the new pole was thicker than the original so the box would not slide down far enough. It came to rest 3 metres (9 feet) above the ground — and there it remained!

All Fall Down

A t an exhibition in Harrogate, England, in 1968 a large display area completely collapsed. The exhibition was organized by the Royal Society for the Prevention of Accidents!

Escape into Captivity

Fifty prisoners in a Mexican jail decided to escape. They planned everything down to the last detail and then began digging an escape tunnel. When the tunnel was finished, they scrambled down into it and came up in the courtroom where they had been sentenced!

Too Many

The Royal couple were General, Sir John Kerr, and the Prime Minister Mr Malcolm Fraser and about 3000 people including 18 busloads of school children.

(*Cape Town Argus*)

A Mistake on the Floor

O ne day in 1861, a worker in a factory forgot to put the lid on a pot of paint. The following day, Frederick Walton, the factory-owner's son, discovered the paint and noticed that a hard skin had formed on the surface. He experimented with this and eventually produced the world's first lino floor-covering.

Wrong Place

J ohn Nash, an amateur weather-forecaster, predicted that the city of Adelaide, Australia, would be engulfed by a tidal wave. He was so sure of this forecast that he moved from Adelaide to a town called Warwick, which he said was the safest place in Australia. A month later, there was heavy flooding – in Warwick.

Power Cut

Local councils always try to save money where they can. But sometimes their plans are not as successful as they hope. This was certainly the case in 1974 when Bramber Parish Council switched off the street lights for three days, as a money-saving exercise.

They saved £11.58. Later, they discovered that it had cost £18.48 to switch the electricity off and an additional £12 for putting it back on again! Instead of saving money the exercise had added £18.90 to the council's costs!

Fishy Accident

Two lanes of the M5 motorway near Cullompton, Devon, in England, were closed in August, 1986. By accident, a lorry had scattered 7 tonnes of sprats along a 3-mile stretch of the motorway.

Fire Raiser

I t is said that accidents always come in threes. That was certainly the case with David Knowlson, of Bristol, England in 1985. First, a slice of bread got stuck in the toaster and filled the kitchen with smoke. The second accident happened when he burned a fir tree in his fireplace – and set the chimney alight. David and his wife Elisabeth were so concerned with that fire they allowed the third accident to happen. They forgot there were some chicken pieces under the grill and the kitchen was filled with smoke once again.

Firemen who were putting out the chimney fire also tackled the flaming chicken and peace reigned once more. David offered the firemen a cup of tea but they declined. They got out quickly before anything else happened!

Expensive Cuppa

When he had finished work for the day in the television shop in Nottingham, England, John Lunt decided to have a cup of tea before going home.

When the shop manager, Tony Sheehan, opened the shop the following day he had the shock of his life. The place was flooded. John had forgotten to turn the tap off and some tea towels had fallen into the sink causing a blockage. There was water everywhere! That cup of tea had caused £12 000 worth of damage.

Snow Joke

Heavy snow is not uncommon in New York, but in one blizzard, motorists got more than they bargained for. Because the snow was so deep, they were forced to abandon their cars. When they returned later to dig them out, they found they had parking tickets attached to their car windscreens.

The Bubble that Burst

I t was a crazy idea but David Kirke and Hugo Spower thought it would be fun to roll down the River Thames inside a huge air balloon! The balloon, nicknamed Melonball, had wires attached to it and was to be pulled along the surface of the river by a tug.

But things did not go according to plan. After only five minutes, the wires snapped, making a hole in the balloon. The two men were almost smothered as the plastic skin fell around them. Luckily, they had advised the river police of their venture and they came to the rescue. They slashed open the skin of Melonball and the two men scrambled aboard a police launch to safety.

Food for Thought

Three masked robbers were lying in wait in a supermarket car-park in New York, when Howard Selley and Wilfred Parsons, two supermarket employees, emerged from the store carrying a plastic bag. The robbers donned their masks, pointed their guns and demanded that the two men hand over the morning's takings.

The two men were surprised by the raid, but handed over the bag. The robbers were even more surprised when they looked in the bag later — it contained apples and cheese sandwiches which the two men had been planning to have for a midday snack.

Top Rates

When people in Leatherhead, England, received their rates bills one year, they telephoned the council to complain. The rates were 100 times higher than normal. It turned out that the council computer had made a mistake in its calculations.

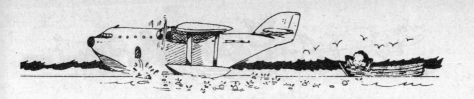

Someone Can't Count

A writer for *Weekend* magazine slipped up when he wrote: 'If you asked six friends to name the commonest bird in Britain, the odds are that nine out of ten would say the sparrow.'

Daguerre's Discovery

L ouis Daguerre (1787-1851) was the inventor of a photographic process for making a metal plate retain an image that could be fixed. One day, while he was working on this process, he left some under-exposed photographic plates in a cupboard. He had forgotten that there was a dish of mercury in there.

The mercury affected the plates and brought out the image on them. As a result of his mistake, Daguerre discovered a new, faster way to develop photographic plates.

All at Sea

Sir Henry Bessemer, famous for his invention of a new steel-making process, always felt seasick when he travelled by ship so he designed a ship that he thought would not make people feel ill. The centre of the vessel was to be made so that it could swing independently from the rest of the ship. Therefore, when the ship rolled in heavy seas, the centre portion could remain level and the passengers would not be affected by the vessel's motion.

A steamer of this design was built and called the *Bessemer* but, when it was tested, the centre portion rolled more than an ordinary vessel. Sir Henry then added a hydraulic brake to be operated by a man who sat watching a spirit level, linked to the centre portion of the ship. Each time the ship rolled, the man would apply the brake just the right amount to keep the centre portion level. This proved even worse than before so the centre portion was fixed and the vessel was used like a conventional ship.

But the vessel's problems were far from over. It was almost unsteerable. On its first trip it crashed into the pier at Calais. It then returned to Dover, hit the pier there and was withdrawn from service.

Photo Fit

During a raid on a house in the north of England, two burglars found a camera and, just for a laugh, they took photographs of themselves. But they dropped the camera getting away from the house. When the film was later developed, the police did not take long to find the culprits.

Late Post

The British Post Office prides itself on the fact that most of its postal deliveries are made quickly. But sometimes they slip up — as they did with a postcard sent to Mrs Marjorie Witts of Harford Court, Sketty, Swansea in 1922. The postman delivered it in June, 1986 — 64 years late! Unfortunately, Mrs Witts had moved from that address 50 years previously!

Iron Lady

What Mrs Thatcher's closest friends are wondering is whether, as the signs suggest, she is beginning to suffer from metal fatigue.

(*The Guardian*)

Cake-Mix Mix-Up

Prima, a magazine for women, often features delicious recipes. In the November 1986 edition, as Christmas was approaching, it included such favourites as Christmas pudding and Christmas cake.

People who tried to make the Christmas cake ended up with a thick sludge which cooled into an inedible lump. The reason for this was a simple printer's error in the recipe. The amounts of butter and sugar were wrong.

As the recipe also included brandy, the people who tried to make the cake spent a lot of money on ingredients, only to have a disaster on their hands. As can be imagined, plenty of them wrote to the magazine demanding compensation.

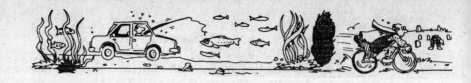

Whacky Wedding

E verything went wrong at Mark Nightingale's wedding to Helen Lennox at Newbury, Berkshire in England, in November, 1985.

When the groom and the best man arrived at the church it was locked and there was no sign of the priest. Guests began arriving but the church remained locked. Five minutes before the ceremony was due to start, the Reverend Leslie Drayer arrived on his bicycle — his car had broken down.

Before the service began, Mark asked his best man to check he had the rings. They had disappeared. When the bride arrived, most of the guests were searching the churchyard for the missing rings.

The couple borrowed two silver rings from Mark's sister and the wedding proceeded as planned. The missing rings were found in a flower bed a few days later.

Hospital Howler

A disc jockey working for a trial period with the BBC read out a dedication to someone in hospital. He then said, 'I think it would be nice to play this record for everyone who is in hospital at the moment. I hope it cheers you up.' Unfortunately, the next record due to be played was called *When I'm Dead and Gone*.

Safe Seal

B urglars at Chichester, Sussex in England slipped up slightly in August, 1980. They used cutting equipment to attack a safe in the leisure centre but they succeeded only in welding up the door. It took the manager of the leisure centre over an hour to get the safe opened the following day.

Just the Ticket

Motorists in Naples, Italy were pleased when traffic wardens put parking tickets on vehicles parked outside the City Hall. The vehicles were police tow-away trucks.

Christmas Call

Father Christmas was his usual busy self in December, 1986. But when he visited Oake Village School near Taunton, Somerset in England, he nearly missed the school party. He arrived early so he hid in a cupboard until it was time to hand out the presents. No one knew he was hiding and while the children were having tea, someone locked the cupboard!

Luckily there was a telephone in the cupboard so Father Christmas called the operator and told her what had happened. At first the operator thought he was joking but eventually she agreed to call the school. The headmaster, Mark Smith, opened the cupboard and Father Christmas stepped out, just in time to give out the presents.

Coin Catch

One of the exhibits in a museum in South Shields, England, was a Roman coin said to be dated between AD 135 and AD 138. But nine-year-old Fiona Gordon was not impressed by it. On seeing the coin she declared it to be nothing but a plastic token. Museum officials were amused by the young girl. But when they checked again they found that the young girl was right. The coin bore a Roman-style design but was definitely made of plastic. The letter R on the coin, which the experts had taken to mean Roma, was in fact the initial letter of a soft-drink manufacturer!

Lift to the Wedding

The bride, who was carried by her father, wore a white, satin dress.

(Craven Herald and Pioneer)

Train Fall

Staff of Pickfords, a carrier firm, had red faces for a day in July, 1975. They were transporting a 23-metre (75-foot)-long hover-train from Erith, in southern England to the Cranfield Technology Institute in Bedfordshire. During its journey it had to negotiate a sharp bend. But the bend proved too sharp and the train fell off the lorry! It remained stranded in a field for 24 hours before a crane was brought to lift it back on to the lorry.

Death Wish

When newspapers mistakenly carried his obituary, the writer, Mark Twain, said, 'Reports of my death have been greatly exaggerated.' A similar thing happened to a man in Scotland. A report in the *Aberdeen Evening Express* said: 'It is with regret we learn of the sudden death of Donald Everett, of Durris, and wish him an early return to full health.'

Letter Catch

Gunman, William Lindley, robbed a bank in Lithia Springs, Georgia, USA. He handed the cashier a note demanding money, but he made one mistake. The note was written on an envelope — and the envelope had his name and address written on it!

Money Well Spent

An engineer in Stockholm, Sweden, thought he was doing very well when he received a number of extremely high salary cheques. Then the Stockholm council, for whom he had been working, checked their computer and realized that it had made a mistake. It had entered the engineer's salary as the equivalent of £7 100 000 per year instead of only £7100!

Life Line

Four people in a light aeroplane crashed in the Sahara desert. For four days they waited for help and then a French Air Force plane spotted them. Some equipment was dropped to them by parachute and they all rushed over to where it fell. They had been dropped a rubber dinghy.

Pop Clangers

When the Decca record company first listened to a group called The Beatles their company executive, Dick Rowe, said, 'We don't like their sound. Groups with guitars are on the way out.'

Other major record companies also rejected the group. They were eventually taken on by a small record company, Parlophone, and went on to be the biggest stars the pop world has ever known.

Bungling Bandits

Bungling bandits must have been very annoyed when they tried to rob a factory in Staffordshire, England in November, 1979. First they attacked a safe without realizing that it was not even locked. Then they failed to turn on the oxygen on their cutting equipment so the hot acetylene flame did not cut but simply melted a hole in the front of the safe. And then one of the robbers put his hand through the hole but could not find any money – the safe was empty!

What a Gas!

I n 1986, shares in British Gas were made available to the public. Thirteen-year-old Martin Young received 800 shares and a cheque for £600 in December, 1986. He was very surprised for he had not applied for any shares and was definitely not owed £600 for an unsuccessful application.

British Gas blamed a computer error for the mix-up and also admitted that almost 50 other people had also been sent shares and cheques by mistake.

Meter Muck-up

P atrick Maxwell of County Tyrone, Northern Ireland was fined £25 in 1982 for fiddling his electricity meter. His crime came to light because he had blundered. He had adjusted the meter the wrong way and given himself a bill of £600!

Explosion in Rome

When he arrived in New York after a flight from Rome on 2 October, 1985, General James Brown found a telegram waiting for him. It was from the Rome police telling him that they had blown up his car.

When the general made enquiries he found the telegram to be true. The chauffeur who had driven the general to Rome airport had parked the car near the ticket office of a foreign airline. Police, always on the lookout for terrorists, believed that the car could contain a bomb. They discovered that the number plate of the car was false and they feared the worst. They then had the car blown up.

Apparently the false number plates had been put on the car for security purposes – but no one on the general's staff had thought to inform the local police.

The Magic Earring

I t is very easy to make a mistake when making a film. In *The King and I*, for example, Yul Brynner, who plays the king, is seen wearing an earring in some shots in a scene, but in other shots the earring has mysteriously disappeared!

Timely Catch

A West German shoplifter shinned down a drainpipe to escape police. He then climbed over a high wall and leapt into the yard below. Unfortunately it was the yard of Dusseldorf Jail. Warders found stolen watches in his pockets, and he ended up doing time.

What a Sauce!

Two dogs approached the fence that Colin Steptoe was creosoting at his landlady's house in Taunton, England. Colin did not take too much notice of the dogs until they started to lick the fence. Then he realized he was using brown sauce instead of creosote!

Bus Bloomer

It was to be a great day for New York, USA, when, in 1977, eight British double-decker buses were to be put into service. But when the buses arrived it was discovered that they were all too tall to be used. No one had thought to check the heights of tunnels, bridges or overhead wires on the proposed routes.

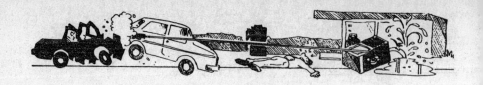

Fortune in a Plastic Bag

John and Nita Askew of Bromley in Kent, England, couldn't believe their eyes when they opened the carrier bag they had found near their home. It was full of fabulous jewellery and gold coins. They took the bag to the police station where it was discovered that it belonged to a local banker.

The banker did not even know the bag was missing. He had taken the bag out of his car to rearrange some other items in the boot and had then forgotten about it. He drove off leaving a fortune by the roadside.

Strip Tease

The clerks at a bank in Texas, USA, had quite a job on their hands. Thanks to a computer error 200 000 incoming cheques had been shredded. The clerks had to sort out a large pile of thin strips of paper to put the cheques back together!

A Wheel Dilemma

As Sharon Dawes and Philip O'Connor were driving home, in Swansea, Wales, after a romantic evening together, they talked of marriage. 'What size ring do you need?' asked Philip. Sharon replied, 'About this size,' and pushed her finger into a hole in the sports-type steering wheel of her car.

And then she found she couldn't get her finger out!

She managed to drive to her home where she tried to get her finger out using butter and grease, but to no avail. Eventually Philip unbolted the steering wheel and took Sharon to the local fire-station where the wheel was cut off with a hacksaw.

Robber in the Dark

Art Eastman waited until everyone had left the shop before he went in to rob the owner. He took out a gun, pulled down his home-made mask and charged into the shop. But he had overlooked one thing when planning the raid – he had forgotton to put eye-holes in the mask – and he couldn't see a thing. As he stumbled around in the dark he pushed up his mask to see where he was and the shopkeeper was later able to give a perfect description.

Wrong Number

A lot of work went into the compilation of the new Paris telephone directory issued in January, 1983. The French Telecommunications Ministry was proud of its efforts – until it was pointed out that they had put down the wrong telephone number for themselves!

The No-stop Stop

David Lashbrooke and his friend, John Henderson, were waiting for a train at Hamble Station near Southampton, England, one Sunday in January, 1983. The train duly arrived and the boys were about to get on, when the guard put his head out of the window and stopped them. 'You can't get on,' he said. 'We don't stop here on Sundays. We only stopped to tell you we don't stop.'

Chain Letter

In 1983, people in Newbury, England received letters from Ireland. The letters were posted in Downpatrick, County Down but all they contained were £10 and £20 notes and nothing else.

A police spokesman said, 'It appears someone is trying to start a chain letter but has forgotten to enclose the instructions.'

Swallow That!

Con-man Peter Lazardes, came up with a good idea. He stole some diamonds and then swallowed them. When it was discovered that the stones were missing no one thought to search Lazardes because it was obvious that he was not concealing anything.

But he did not get away with the crime. The stones were discovered, still lodged in his stomach, when he died six months later.

Pin-up Puzzler

One day, during the English Cup Final week, both *The Sun* and *The Star* newspapers featured photographs of pin-up, Corinne Russell. The caption in *The Sun* said she supported Brighton, but according to *The Star* she was a Manchester United fan. In the event, neither newspaper got it right. 'I'm not the least bit interested in football,' said Corinne.

Rent Arrears

A 63-year-old widow received quite a shock when she had a letter from the council saying that she faced eviction for non-payment of rent. She had lived in the house at Chingford, in Essex, England, for 19 years and had always been prompt in paying her rent. When she approached the council she discovered the amount of her arrears — one penny.

Gun Alarm

W hen the man sitting opposite pulled a gun from his pocket, the lady traveller screamed and pulled the communication cord. The train shuddered to a halt and the guard came to investigate — only to find a very embarrassed young lady. The gun was a water pistol that the man had just bought for his son.

Tourist's Troubles

A tourist once spent three days exploring 'the delights of Rome'. What he did not realize was that he had got off the plane too early when it had stopped to re-fuel. It was three days before he discovered that he was actually in New York!

Hospital Stay

In 1953 Mrs Alice Coe went to visit her aunt in a mental hospital in Jamestown, Virginia, USA. When she got there she was told that her aunt had died, but she was very welcome to see the room she had occupied. Mrs Coe went to the room and, as she was tired after her journey, she lay down on the bed for a nap.

She woke up when a doctor came into the room and told her she was to be transferred to another room. Mrs Coe went with the doctor to the other room. She stayed in the hospital for 25 years before the mistake was discovered and she was eventually discharged.

Marriage Mix-up

Albert Muldoon was the best man at the wedding in Kileter, County Tyrone in Northern Ireland but no one had told him where he should stand. He stood next to the bride, so the priest assumed he was the groom and addressed all the questions to him. It was only after the service, when they went to sign the register that the priest discovered he had married the best man to the bride. The ceremony had to be conducted again, this time with the groom and the best man in the correct places.

This is a Zip Up

Robber, Raymond Burles, walked into a Paris bank, brandishing a gun, and ordered the cashiers to put money in his bag. Then he zipped up the bag and ordered everyone to stay where they were as he backed out of the bank. But no one took any notice. Instead of standing still, with their hands up, they jumped on him, and called the police. The people in the bank were no longer afraid of him as he had put the gun in the bag by mistake.

Transport Trip-up

In 1968, executives of the Long Island Railway in New York were delighted with the new 100-mph trains they had bought, until they found out that the trains were too big to go through the tunnel leading to the Brooklyn terminals. They were also the wrong size for the railway platforms!

Car Crazy

Motoring organizations such as the British Automobile Association help drivers who call in to say they have broken down. A woman once telephoned the AA to say that her car would not go faster than 30 mph and that she had used 245 litres (54 gallons) of petrol on a journey from London to Bodmin in Cornwall, a distance of 240 miles.

A patrolman was sent out to investigate but he could find nothing wrong with the car. He asked the driver if the gears were causing any problems. 'Gears?' asked the lady. 'What gears?' She had been used to driving an automatic car and had driven the whole journey in first gear!

One Day Daily

A new British national newspaper, the *Commonwealth Sentinel* was launched on 6 February 1965. It was founded by Lionel Burleigh for all Commonwealth citizens. Mr Burleigh had done everything he could to ensure that the newspaper would be successful, and he had done a great deal of work. He had written most of the stories, collected the advertisements and supervised the printing.

On the day of the launch Mr Burleigh was relaxing in his London hotel room when the police called. They were concerned by the fact that 50 000 copies of the *Commonwealth Sentinel* had been dumped outside the hotel. Mr Burleigh had produced the paper on time but he had forgotten to arrange for its distribution! None of the newspapers reached the newsagents and the *Commonwealth Sentinel* was never published again.

Hiccup at Heathrow

On 14 October, 1985, the British Prime Minister, Mrs Margaret Thatcher, went to Heathrow Airport to greet the Indian Prime Minister, Rajiv Gandhi, at the start of his two-day visit to Britain. While waiting for Mr Gandhi's plane to arrive, Mrs Thatcher bent down to pat a police dog. The Alsatian, named Ultra, quickly grabbed one of Mrs Thatcher's gloves. No matter how sternly the Prime Minister requested the return of her glove, Ultra just sat there with the glove held firmly between his jaws.

Eventually, Constable Bob Bourne, the dog's handler came to the rescue. He managed to recover the glove and it was smoothed out just in time for Mrs Thatcher to put it on for Mr Gandhi's arrival.

Funfair Fanfare

During the Second World War, King Haakon of Norway visited the BBC studios in London to make a broadcast to his people. It had been decided to open the programme with a magnificent fanfare. But someone in the sound library misread the instructions as 'funfair' and the programme opened with a fairground barker crying 'Roll up, roll up. All the fun of the fair!'

Behind the Scenes

The Oliviers make one of their rear appearances together on British television.
(*Daily Express*)

Too Good to be True

A West-German crook once found that it does not pay to be too good at one's job. He devised a way of forging 5-Deutschmark coins – but the coins he produced were just too perfect and it was not long before he was detected.

Fleming's Find

One day in 1928, scientist, Alexander Fleming, found some mould growing in a dish in which he had set up an experiment with bacteria. He noticed that the bacteria were not reproducing in an area around the mould. He went on to do experiments with the mould and eventually developed the valuable medicine, penicillin. It was purely by accident that one of the greatest ever wonder drugs was discovered.

Lost Results

A BBC commentator presenting the sports report was heard to say, 'Nowhere are the football results.' There was an embarrassed silence and then he spoke again: 'I'm sorry, I'll read that again. Now here are the football results.'

Wrestler who Beat Himself

A merican wrestler, Stanley Pinto, got tangled up in the ropes during one of his bouts. In his attempts to get out he put his shoulders on the mat for three seconds – and was declared the loser. His opponent was nowhere near him at the time.

Thanks for Nothing

R obert Wilson, a solicitor from Windsor, England, received a tax demand for £0.00 with instructions that he had to pay before January, 1975. Mr Wilson duly obeyed the instruction and sent off his cheque for £0.00. A few days later he received a receipt for £0.00 sent by first class post.

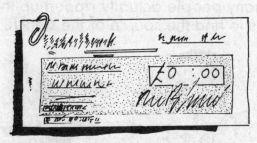

That Takes the Biscuit

H untley and Palmers, the British biscuit manufacturers, were pleased with the tins they had designed for the Christmas market. They showed elegant ladies sipping tea at an old-fashioned tea party. Thousands of tins had gone out to the shops before it was discovered that there were also several rather rude drawings mixed in the scene. The tins are now collectors' items.

Phew!

To help detect any possible gas leaks, workmen injected a foul-smelling gas into the gas mains in New York, USA. It seemed like a good idea at the time but, unfortunately, the workmen never thought to tell anyone about their brilliant idea. As a result, gas officials received numerous complaints about the smell and many people actually ripped up their floor-boards to find the source of the stench.

Wet Test

During her driving test in Guildford, England, Mrs Beatrice Park accidentally put her foot on the accelerator instead of the brake. Unfortunately, this happened in Riverside Way. The car crashed through some railings and ended up in the River Wey. Mrs Park and her instructor had to be rescued by boat.

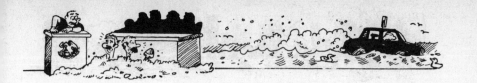

Atomic Disaster

E arly in October, 1976, Viennese radio, in Austria gave out a frightening message: 'Disaster at atomic power station – catastrophe warning. An atomic cloud driven by the wind is moving slowly towards the city.' Parents rushed to schools to pick up their children; telephone lines were jammed and people panicked to escape the approaching horror.

But it was all a mistake. The power station at Zwentendorf, 30 miles away, had not even started operations. The radio message was simply an exercise to find out what would happen if such a disaster were to occur.

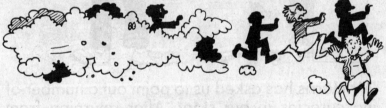

Pepsi Clanger

E xecutives of the Pepsi Cola company thought they would do well in Germany with their famous advertising phrase 'Come alive with Pepsi'. But they nearly slipped up for the translation into German read, 'Come out of the grave with Pepsi.'

Newspaper Apology

Two English local newspapers, the *Wiltshire Times* and *Chippenham News*, once carried a feature about a local man called Mr Harris. But the following week they had to print this apology:

'Mr Harris has asked us to point out a number of inaccuracies in our story. After returning from India, he served in Ireland for four years and not six months as stated; he never farmed at Heddington, particularly not at Coate Road Farm as stated; he has never counted cycling or walking among his hobbies; he is not a member of 54 hunts; and he did not have an eye removed after an air raid on Calne.'

Crime Doesn't Pay

I n 1978, a team of crooks in Shepton Mallet, England, tried to do six robberies, but ended up with nothing. They smashed a window to get into a solicitor's office but one of them cut his finger badly and the crooks had to go home. Next, they broke into a house by climbing a drainpipe and getting in through an upstairs window, only to find that the house was empty and up for sale. At a garage they ripped open the top of a filing cabinet before they discovered it was not locked and only contained files of paper. When they broke into the local council planning office they found nothing to steal. They then broke into a boutique and then an auctioneer's rooms and on both occasions found that there was nothing worth stealing.

No Way to Cross

Road-builders in County Galway in southern Ireland once built a much-needed road to join two villages, Cornamona and Crimlin. There was only one snag — no one had thought to plan for a bridge over the river that ran between the two villages. And so, when the road was finished, the two sections went as far as the river — and stopped! Drivers had to get out and walk across the river on stepping stones!

The Last Bus?

A health authority in West Germany once objected to a description of one of the local bus company's routes. On the front of the buses the route was described as: 'The cemetery via the hospital'.

False Fire

On 18 December, 1985, the driver of a coach driving along the M1 motorway near Milton Keynes, Buckinghamshire suddenly felt very ill and had to stop. He had dined with his passengers and had eaten too much. As none of the passengers were able to drive the coach, one of them rushed to a telephone and called the police saying, 'Our coach driver has over-eaten.'

Unfortunately there was a lot of interference on the telephone line and the policeman on the other end thought the man had said, 'Our coach is over heating.'

Within minutes, 20 firemen were rushing to the scene and police were preparing to block off the motorway in case the coach caught fire. When the firemen arrived they found a rather embarrassed coach driver and a coachload of confused passengers.

Nosey

T he attempt at burglary backfired when security guards heard the nose of a fruit machine being forced.

(Middlesbrough Evening Gazette)

The Tooth of the Matter

W hen he escaped fom Nevada State Prison, USA, convict, Clive Castro, believed he had thought of everything. But he had forgotten one detail – he'd left his false teeth behind in prison. After only three days of freedom he was longing for his favourite meal of grilled steak and onions. But without any teeth there was no way he could eat it. There was only one thing to do – he gave himself up so that he could get back to his teeth.

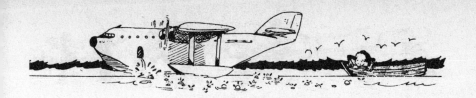

Soft Landing

I t was no real surprise to the British flying boat crew that the air vice-marshal wanted to inspect their craft. (Flying boats, in use during the first half of this century, were aircraft that took off from and landed on water.) After take-off, the air vice-marshal asked if he could take the controls. Everything went well until the air vice-marshal prepared to land at an airfield on the Isle of Wight near the south coast of England. One of the crew looked at the oncoming runway and politely reminded the air vice-marshal that an airfield landing would not be appropriate.

The air vice-marshal took the hint and headed towards the stretch of water called The Solent where he touched down. He then thanked the crewman for reminding him that he was flying a flying boat before opening the door and calmly stepping out!

Crazy Treaty

The agreement to end the First World War was signed in November, 1918. But the signatories did not notice, until afterwards, the mistake made by the man who had typed the document. He had put some of the sheets of carbon paper into the typewriter the wrong way round and as a result, some sections of the important document were back to front.

Absorbing Discovery

Aworker at a paper-mill in Berkshire, England in the 19th century forgot to add sizing materials to the paper he was making. The resultant paper was unsuitable as writing paper as it soaked up ink. Then it was realized that this new, absorbent paper could be used for drying up ink – and blotting paper was born!

Stamp of Stupidity

Many years ago, a London stamp collector sent two 2½p stamps to the Post Office to pay for the postage on a first day cover he wanted. In fact, he should have sent two 3p stamps. The Post Office sent him a telegram asking for the 1p. The telegram cost 40p.

Wet Launch

Miss May Gould was asked to launch a ship in Boston, Massachusetts, USA. When she tried to hit the vessel with the traditional bottle of champagne the bottle missed but the ship slid away down the slipway.

Miss Gould was not going to leave the vessel un-named. She ran along the pier, dived into the water, smashed the bottle against the ship and named it from there.

Horse Laugh

He gave an example of a problem quite near his home where a large horse had been empty for years eight years, and it had a local authority mortgage.

(*Ashborne News Telegraph*)

Handy Cover-Up

A burglar in the USA thought he had a good idea. He took his socks off and wore them on his hands so as not to leave any fingerprints. But police in Chattanooga, Tennessee arrested him soon after. They identified him by his footprints!

Wine from the Ashes

Some mishaps have a happy ending. The fire that raged across the island of Madeira in the 14th century is one such incident. At that time, Madeira was covered in thick woodland. The fire, which started by accident, raged for seven years leaving nothing but a thick layer of ash over the land. The settlers then did the best they could with the land and planted some vines. It was not long before they were harvesting a bumper crop, and Madeira wine became famous all over the world.

The Hunter Hunted

Hungarian hunter, Endre Bascany, was an expert at imitating the love-call of a stag. Unfortunately, he was too good. One day in 1976 a hunter heard his call, thought it was a stag and fired, shooting Bascany in the arm.

Safe Safe

Police raced to the scene when it was reported that a safe had been dumped by a roadside. Try as they might the police could not move the safe, so they called for more equipment. For an hour they guarded the safe until the equipment arrived.

But even the extra equipment did not help. The safe still would not budge. And then the truth dawned. The 'safe' was not a safe after all. It was an electricity junction-box and it was securely cemented into the ground.

Difficult Exercise

A South African newspaper once suggested an exercise to keep fit. It was rather difficult. The instructions were: 'Lie flat on the back, with the feet tucked under the wardrobe. Keep the hands at the sides and raise the legs until they are vertical.'

Late Apology

O n 9 June, 1986, The Worshipful Company of Bakers, one of the famous guilds of London, officially apologized for a blunder made by one of their profession 320 years before.

The gentleman for whom the guild was apologizing was John Farynor in whose bakery the Great Fire of London started on 2 September, 1666. But he was not the only one to blame. The Lord Mayor and the people of London also blundered by not taking the fire seriously and allowing it to spread. The fire was discovered in the bakery at Pudding Lane at 2am. It spread slowly at first, and as fires were common in London at that time no one took any notice. But the fire began spreading rapidly and eventually destroyed three quarters of the city!

Bungled Burglary

The robbers had planned their burglary of a supermarket in Navan, Eire, down to the last detail. They would climb into an attic at the rear of the building, make a hole in the floor and climb down into the supermarket.

Getting into the attic was fairly easy but when they started to dig a hole in the attic floor it was harder than they had expected. It turned out to be made of reinforced concrete and it took several hours to break through. At long last, the hole was finished and the robbers jumped through — to find themselves outside. They had miscalculated the length of the store.

Ropey Excuse

Eight teams turned up for a tug-of-war contest at Fleet in Lincolnshire, northern England, but the match had to be cancelled — the organizers forgot to bring a rope!

Art Award

The American Academy of Design was so impressed by a painting submitted by Edward Dickenson that they gave him a top art award. They were rather embarrassed to discover that they had conducted their judging with the painting hanging upside down!

Gas Error

South Eastern Gas had received no payment from 57 Dalmally Road, Croydon, near London so they sent their usual final demand. There was still no payment forthcoming so they threatened to cut off the supply if the bill was not paid immediately. That did the trick – a cheque arrived a week later, from South Eastern Gas! The house that had incurred the charges was their own show-house!

Dirty Work

C ontractors were asked by the council of Penistone, near Sheffield, England to clean the stonework on 50 houses. But the council forgot to inform one of the householders, Mrs Robinson. When she first saw the workmen they had already cleaned the lower half of her house. Mrs Robinson said, 'It's taken 35 years to give this house character. I want it to stay dirty.' The contractors offered to clean the rest of the house for nothing but Mrs Robinson was adamant – and the men had to put the dirt back on to the house!

Cow Catastrophe

On October, 1871, in Chicago, a cow belonging to the widow O'Leary became agitated when it heard a noise. It kicked out and knocked a lighted lantern into a bale of hay. Flames soon engulfed the barn. The Chicago fire brigade rushed to the farm but their water soon ran out and it was not long before the flames spread through the city.

The fire raged for 28 hours. The cost of the damage was put at over £75 000 000, and some 2124 acres were devastated.

Language Problem

A Scotsman bought a toy gun and went into a newsagent's shop in Luton, England. He pointed the gun at a girl assistant and said, 'This is a stick up.' But because of his broad Scottish accent, the girl could not understand a word.

'Bang, bang,' said the would-be robber. 'You're dead,' replied the girl, and she burst into a fit of laughter. The robber felt he had no alternative but to leave empty-handed.

Slow Driver

I n 1977, Dr Emil Gruhner reported 50 drivers to the police for overtaking him recklessly on a German autobahn. But a number of drivers had already reported him for driving too slowly on the motorway — 19kmh (12mph).

An Arresting Party

O ver 100 people made a big mistake on 16 December, 1985, when they accepted an invitation to a party in Washington, USA. The party had apparently been arranged by a sports promotion firm offering a slap-up party and free tickets to a football match. What the party goers, all of them wanted by the police, did not know was that the 'sports firm' did not exist and that all the people in fancy dress at the party were police officers. They soon found out, however, when the host who had welcomed them made an announcement: 'We have a special surprise for you. You are under arrest. Put your hands up.'

Football Hero

United goalkeeper, Stepney, went full length to save from Hector and then, in the 18th minute, saved an almost certain goal when he bravely died at the feet of Davies.

(*The Gloucester Citizen*)

Cracked It!

Stage star, Gertrude Lawrence, swung the bottle to launch her cabin cruiser at Southampton in 1934, but the bottle missed. Undeterred, she had another attempt — and the ribbon broke. She then took the neck of the bottle in both hands and hit it against the bows of the vessel. Still, the bottle did not break. Finally, she got an axe to smash open the bottle and the cruiser was launched successfully.

Carpet Catastrophe

T he young couple were very pleased with the length of carpet they bought at a jumble sale in Derbyshire, England, in 1985. But the town clerk of Bakewell was not too pleased about it for the carpet belonged to the town hall! Members of St. Giles's Church in the village of Great Longstone had thought the carpet was jumble so they put it in their sale for just £1. They were not to know that the rolled-up carpet was only used in Bakewell town hall to deaden the sound of footsteps when the magistrate's court was sitting.

A notice was displayed outside the town hall and an advertisement placed in the local newspaper. A week later the couple who had bought the carpet telephoned — but by that time they had cut it to fit their staircase!

The Car That Was No-go

For a long time, General Motors had been having no success with their Nova Chevrolet in South America.

It was pointed out at last that the advertising men had forgotten one important point. 'No-va' in colloquial Spanish means 'won't go'.

Fingerprint

American gangster, John Dillinger, knew his fingerprints were on the files of the FBI (Federal Bureau of Investigation). He thought it would be a good idea if he got some new fingerprints so he put the tips of his thumbs and fingers in acid to remove his old ones. He endured weeks of agony until his skin healed. But when he compared his new fingerprints with his old ones they were exactly the same!

Secret Weapon

During the Second World War, a new weapon called the Panjandrum was invented. It consisted of two 3-metre (10-foot)-high wheels joined by an axle. Around each wheel were rocket charges designed to propel the wheels forward over land and sea.

The Panjandrum was built in absolute secret in Leytonstone, England. Part way through its construction, it was realized that the building in which it was being made was going to be too small to house it! One wall of the shed had to be removed so that the construction work could continue.

That was not the only blunder. The Panjandrum was tested on the beach at Westward Ho, Devon, in September, 1943. The machine was placed in the sea and the rockets ignited. But one rocket fell off and the machine turned around and headed in the wrong direction.

A further test was arranged for the following day. This time the Panjandrum covered about 365 metres (400 yards), twice as far as on the first test before getting itself bogged down in some sand.

Adjustments were made to the machine and a third wheel, carrying more rockets, was added but the rockets failed to ignite!

During the months that followed, more adjustments were made and more tests were carried out — but without success. The final test came in January, 1944, when high-ranking officers were invited to watch this amazing new secret weapon in action. Everything went wrong. Some rockets fell off and the Panjandrum careered wildly out of control. Before long it was heading towards the officers who had come to watch and they had to run for their lives! Then it turned and headed out to sea where it disintegrated completely. After that the project was abandoned!

Parrot Power

In 1975, Pamela Johnson made the mistake of putting her parrot, Charlie, in his cage on top of the cooker while she went out. When she had gone, Charlie put his claw out and turned on the hotplate control of the cooker. Seconds later, the paper on the floor of his cage burst into flames. Charlie opened the cage door and flew out, just in time to save himself from a roasting.

When Pamela arrived home, she saw a heap of charred rubbish at the bottom of the cage. She believed that Charlie had cooked himself until she heard a voice behind her saying, 'Naughty Charlie, naughty Charlie.'

Birthday Boob

Tony Blackburn, the British disc-jockey, once played a record for a man who was celebrating his 70th birthday. But, without checking first, he played — *Knockin' On Heaven's Door*!

Miserable Wedding

Barclays Bank mounted an expensive advertising campaign to attract newly-weds to bank with them. The advertisements, which cost £1 750 000, showed a clergyman marrying a young couple — but the model who played the vicar was dressed in the robes used for a funeral!

Too Late

Most crooks plan their crimes down to the last detail, but sometimes they can miss important points. This was certainly the case with three thieves who set out to rob a sub post office at Billericay, Essex in England.

They leapt out of their car brandishing shotguns. But they had overlooked one important point — the post office had closed 12 years before.

Eggsplosion

C onstable Kevin Doherty was having a boiled egg during a break from motorway duty early one morning in December, 1985. As he dipped his spoon into the egg there was a terrific explosion that rocked the tiny canteen at Charnock Richard, near Preston, Lancashire, England. At first several of his colleagues thought they had been victims of a terrorist attack but it turned out to be a basic blunder by Constable Doherty. He had boiled his egg but when he started eating it he found it was undercooked so he put it in a microwave oven for a few seconds and then tried it again.

One thing that should never be cooked in a microwave is an egg in its shell, even if the top has been taken off. Enormous pressure builds up inside the egg and it was the release of this pressure when the policeman pushed his spoon into the egg that caused the explosion.

Bottoms Up

Ray Howarth will never forget the day in 1985 that he decided to go for a swim in the River Ouse at York, England. He did not have a swimming costume with him so he stripped down to his underpants and dived in. But as he entered the water he lost his underpants. For ten embarrassing minutes he swam up and down not daring to leave the water, as a cheering crowd had gathered. Eventually a policeman arrived, found Ray's trousers and persuaded him to come out of the water.

Icy Road

During a bout of particularly cold weather in January, 1987, a woman drove along an icy road in Chester, England, looking for Canal Street. Several people waved at her as she passed. She thought they were just being friendly until she realized they were trying to tell her something. She was driving on the frozen surface of the Shropshire Union Canal! She leapt out of the Mini and ran to the bank, just in time to see her car sink through the ice into 2.5 metres (8 feet) of water.

Caught by a Lamp-post

Two criminals who made a dash for freedom from an English court in 1985 made just one mistake. They forgot they were handcuffed together and ran either side of a lamp-post! The police had no trouble in recapturing the stunned pair.

Dog Dialler

When police in Humberside, England, answered an emergency call in September, 1985, they were concerned to hear moaning and groaning on the line. They asked the caller to give a name but it seemed obvious that he or she was not in a fit state to do so. Telephone engineers traced the call to a house in Bridlington but when police arrived there it was locked.

They traced the owner, Nick Clarke, at work and rushed him home. He expected to find his wife ill or injured but when he entered the house his anguish turned to embarrassment. Domino, his dog, greeted him as he entered. In the dog's mouth was what was left of the telephone receiver! While chewing it he had accidentally dialled for emergency services.

AMAZING

HOAXES
AND
FRAUDS

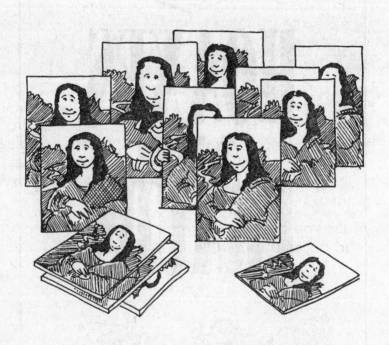

Introduction

Would you have booked a sun-filled holiday on the island of Sans Seriffe or the land of Couani? Would you have voted for Yetta Bronstein in the US Presidential elections or for the *Miss Radio One* Beauty Contest?

If you had – then, you would have been *had*! For these are some of the outrageous hoaxes that have been played – with great success – on countless unsuspecting victims. This book includes over 150 of the most hilarious hoaxes and ingenious frauds ever perpetrated: April Fools, devastating con tricks, cunning masquerades, practical jokes, great art forgeries and literary spoofs.

Could you have been taken in by any of these? Read on, and find out just how gullible you are!

Get Your Hat Cut

In 1980, the British newspaper, the *Daily Express* published a feature on how Guardsmen have to have their famous busby hats cut. The report said that the fur on the hats continues to grow and has to be cut from time to time. There was even a photograph showing a Guardsman at the busby-barber's shop. Thousands of readers believed the story to be true but it proved to be a hoax.

Sounds Fishy!

Man Eating Fish' said the sign outside a sideshow at a garden fête. To see such a fearsome monster was a chance in a lifetime and people willingly paid the modest entry fee.

But inside, they did not find the denizen of the deep they had expected. All they saw was a man eating a plate of cod and chips!

Football Fakers

Christian Morin, president of Rouen Football Club in France, was overjoyed. The great Brazilian club, Santos, had offered to play Rouen for a very small fee. To play such a prestigious team would be a tremendous boost for the Rouen club.

On the day of the match, in September, 1974, 2000 fans packed the stadium. They knew Rouen did not stand a chance but they wanted to see the great Brazilians in action.

When Rouen scored the first goal the crowd put it down to luck and the fact that Rouen was more used to playing in a muddy field than were Santos. But at the end of the match the score was 10-0, to Rouen.

It was obvious that Christian Morin had been the victim of an expensive practical joke. Not only did Rouen win 10-0, but it was suddenly realized that the Brazilians had been talking French not Portuguese. They turned out to be a team of hoaxers from Belgium. They disappeared, taking their fee with them.

The Wakefield Noctifier

Have you ever seen a noctifier? This strange-looking bird is part bittern and part eagle owl. The only known specimen of this extraordinarily rare species is in the City Museum of Wakefield, Yorkshire. It is, of course, a fake.

Troop Movements

During the Second World War, the Germans kept a close watch on troop movements in the British Isles. They need not have bothered — many of the movements were faked by using dummies as troops.

Italian Genius

Alceo Dossena was so good at forging sculptures that some experts thought his works were better than the originals. In the 1920s, Dossena fakes were to be found in most of the great museums of the world – although curators did not know their prized possessions were clever forgeries. Some of Dossena's works have been discovered and exposed but it is very likely that many of his sculptures are still believed to be genuine.

How Shocking!

The popular silent-film actor, Douglas Fairbanks, loved practical jokes. In his house he had a chair that could give the sitter a small electric shock – not enough to hurt, but sufficient to cause a mild tingle. He loved to see his friends jump out of the chair but on one

occasion it appeared not to work. A young lady had sat in the chair but had not reacted to the electricity. Fairbanks asked her if she had felt anything. 'Yes, Mr Fairbanks,' she said, 'but I thought everyone would feel like that when meeting a famous film star like you.'

Coins in Concrete

In 1970 some men once offered a jeweller in Manchester, England, 5000 gold sovereigns, all encased in cement. The jeweller broke open a few lumps of concrete, which all contained gold coins. Satisfied with this proof, he paid a £5000 deposit for the 2000 pieces of concrete he had been given and the men went off to get the remaining 3000.

When the men did not return, the jeweller began to get worried and he broke open a few more pieces of concrete. Not one of them contained a coin and he realized he had been conned.

137

Men on the Moon

Men on the Moon! We now know that there is no life on the Moon but years ago, many people believed that it could be inhabited.

In 1835, an American newspaper reported that the astronomer, Sir John Herschel, had discovered life on the Moon. The paper said that Sir John was in South Africa testing a powerful new telescope. With this remarkable device he was able to see trees, vegetables, vegetation, oceans, beaches, bisons, goats and pelicans on the lunar surface.

It was later stated that the astronomer had seen people on the Moon. They lived in caves and had long wings attached to their shoulders.

The stories convinced so many people that the Journal of Commerce asked for permission to reproduce the articles in a scientific pamphlet, and it was then that the hoax was revealed.

Both the writer, Richard Adams Locke, and the newspaper, the *New York Sun*, admitted the stories were a hoax. It would certainly have had to have been quite a remarkable telescope to reveal all that!

The Third Eye

Lama Lobsang Rampa wrote a number of successful books about his life in a Tibetan monastery. In the books, he told of a miraculous 'third eye' which he possessed that gave him a unique spiritual insight.

But Lama Lobsang Rampa never existed, neither did the monastery. The books were created by Cyril Henry Hoskins who made a lot of money from them.

Non-existent Houses

In London there are two houses that do not exist. They have been hoaxing people for almost 120 years. Numbers 23 and 24 Leinster Gardens in London's Bayswater look just like two 19th-century terraced houses from the front – but they are fakes. Built in 1868, they consist simply of a frontage and were designed to conceal the presence of an underground railway line which runs beneath the street.

Sorting the Post

I n 1977, Tom Jackson, General Secretary of the British Union of Post Office Workers voiced his protests on a radio programme against the proposal that Britain adopt the German system of addressing envelopes. In this method the house number is written after, not before, the name of the road.

Mr Jackson was furious at the idea, for it would, he said, 'alter a great deal of the way we work in the Post Office. Postal workers would be furious because it would turn upside-down the way we have learned to sort.'

As a result of the broadcast, several people telephoned the BBC to support Mr Jackson in his fight. They were politely reminded of the date – it was 1 April.

The Great Barnum

Before Phineas Taylor Barnum became a great showman, he worked in a store where everything was not quite as it seemed. Almost everything he sold was a fake. 'Everything in that store,' said Barnum, 'was different from what it represented.'

Horse Laugh

The Cambridge University Veterinary Society has an unusual mascot — the skeleton of a centaur. Centaurs, half man and half horse, were believed by the ancients to live in the hills of Greece. The centaur of Cambridge in England is much smaller than the creatures of Greek myth for it is only 60 centimetres (2 feet) long and 60 centimetres high. It is, of course, a fake. It was made from the skeletons of a dog and a monkey.

141

Fool's Gold

A gang fooled people into buying fake gold bars in 1978. In one case, a London restaurant owner was offered 804 bars for £50 000. To make sure the gold was genuine the buyer tested a few bars and they appeared to be all right. It was only when the deal had been completed and the men had gone that he decided to check some more of the bars. They turned out to be made of brass, thinly covered with gold.

Cut-price Con

T he man who went into the tobacconist said he was a detective and showed his identity card to prove it. He then showed the shopkeeper a photograph of a man who was in the area selling cigarettes at less than half price and who was wanted for questioning.

The shopkeeper did not recognize the person in the photograph but, a few minutes later, while the plain-clothes detective was still in the shop, the wanted man came in. As expected, he

offered to sell the shopkeeper some cigarettes at a bargain price. From the far side of the shop the detective indicated to the shopkeeper that he should buy the cigarettes. As soon as the transaction was completed the detective came over and arrested the man. He confiscated the £100 the shopkeeper had handed over for the cigarettes and also took the cigarettes as evidence. The shopkeeper did not see the detective, the wanted man, or his money again.

Heavyweight Actor

In one scene in the film *The Godfather*, the Godfather, played by Marlon Brando, is injured and has to be carried away on a stretcher.

When this scene was being filmed, the actors found they could hardly lift the stretcher. It had suddenly become extremely heavy. Marlon Brando had secretly loaded it with several very heavy weights.

What a Cat-astrophe

Sometimes a hoax can rebound on the hoaxer. This happened to the famous author, Mark Twain. He advertised in a newspaper that he had lost his cat which was 'so black that it could not be seen by ordinary light'. Almost 1000 people called at his house claiming that they had found his invisible cat.

Fire Water

Actress, Joan Sims, thought the scene she was about to film was quite straightforward. But she had reckoned without the jokes of her co-star, Kenneth Williams.

During the scene, she had to drink a glass of water. She had a few choice words to say to Kenneth Williams when they came off the set. He had filled the glass with vodka!

The Stones that Lied

Dr Johann Bartholomew Adam Beringer was an 18th-century German scientist who had a deep interest in fossils. When his staff began finding a great number of marvellously formed fossils on Mount Eivelstadt, near Würzburg, Beringer was overjoyed. In 1726, a year after the first discovery, he wrote a book describing the finds and putting forward his theories as to how they were formed.

Unfortunately, Beringer had fallen victim to a cruel hoax perpetrated by some other scientists who did not like him. The stones, later known as 'lying stones', had been handmade and then buried on the hillside. The hoax ruined Beringer, as had been intended, but when the plot was revealed the scientists were justly punished and remained in disgrace for the rest of their lives.

145

Hogging Attention

People in England flocked to fairs in the 19th century to see some of the amazing things on display. A famous exhibit was the pig-faced lady.

To the gullible people of the time she appeared genuine enough. But the pig-faced lady was in reality a bear, with its face and paws shaved, dressed in women's clothing.

Shakespeare's Lost Play

Samuel Ireland was an 18th-century Englishman who did not think much of his 17-year-old son, William. He considered him to be talentless and fit for nothing. Knowing what his father's views were, William was determined to prove himself to him.

Samuel collected rare books and manuscripts and William decided that the best way to impress him would be to provide him with something for his collection. As Samuel was particularly obsessed by Shakespeare, the young boy decided to forge a letter from Queen Elizabeth I to the playwright. This succeeded in fooling his father completely and William set about making some further 'finds'.

The second forgery was of a lease with William Shakespeare's signature. Samuel Ireland was of course overjoyed when he saw it.

William produced a steady supply of Shakespearian items. He told his father that he had found them in an old chest belonging to a gentleman for whom he had done some work. The old man had given William permission to take what he liked from the chest. William's father believed every word.

The ultimate forgery was to be a complete play by Shakespeare. Titled *Vortigern and Rowena*, it took young William just two months to think of the plot and write it all out.

Vortigern and Rowena was actually performed on the London stage on 2 April, 1796. It was a complete flop and William eventually admitted that it was a forgery. His father, however, refused to believe him and remained convinced that all the finds had been absolutely genuine.

The Politician who Vanished

O n a miserable November day in 1973, John Stonehouse, a British Member of Parliament, disappeared. A pile of his clothes was found on Miami beach, USA, and it was thought that he had drowned while swimming.

This was exactly what Stonehouse had planned. But he had not drowned at all. He had made his way to Australia where he hoped to start a new life. He had already set himself up with two false identities in Australia: Joseph Markham and Donald Mildoon.

Shortly after Stonehouse arrived in Australia, the police began watching him closely. Eventually they realized that he was the missing British politician. They arrested him and he was extradited to Britain in 1975.

On 6 August, 1976, Stonehouse was found guilty of theft, forgery and fraud and was given a seven-year prison sentence.

Delicious

The actor, Oliver Reed, was staying in an American hotel that had a large goldfish tank in its reception area. He secretly obtained a carrot and cut it into the shape of a goldfish. When all attention was on him he walked to the fish tank, put his hand in, brought out the carrot and ate it. It was an old theatrical gag but the management did not appreciate the joke. They ordered the actor to leave the hotel.

Who's Zoo

Zoos around the British Isles dread April Fool's Day. On that day each year they are certain to receive calls from Mr L E Phant, Mr C Lyon, Mrs G Raffe and Mr Albert Ross.

The Man Who Never Was

I n 1943, during the Second World War, the body of Major William Martin was discovered off a Spanish beach. He was buried with full military honours at Huelva in the south-west of Spain.

Documents he had been carrying were returned to London where they were carefully examined. It was obvious that they had been tampered with and that was exactly what the British had hoped would happen, for Major Martin was a hoax designed to fool the Germans.

Major Martin did not exist. The body was that of a man who had died of pneumonia, a death that would appear to be by drowning if the body was recovered from the sea. With the permission of

the man's parents, the body had been put into the sea near Spain in the hope that the Germans would find it and read the fake papers he carried. The papers stated that the Allies would attack Sardinia, when in fact they intended to attack Sicily.

The hoax was successful. When the Allies launched their offensive on Sicily, most of the heavy German equipment had been moved to defend the island of Sardinia.

Hole in the Road

A group of road menders were repairing a street in Manhattan, USA. An official from their head office appeared on the scene and told them to go to another site, a short distance away, and dig a hole. When the hole was a good size, the official returned to his office. It was only then, when the traffic was in chaos all around them, that the workmen realized they had been hoaxed. The 'man from head office' turned out to be Hugh Troy, the famous practical joker.

Caught on the Hop

Callers jammed the switchboard of a local British radio station, Radio Trent, after England cricket player, Derek Randall, had appealed for help in capturing a baby kangaroo. He said it had been a present from a cricket club in Perth. The story was a hoax.

Bonaparte's Baton

The famous French emperor, Napoleon Bonaparte, once presented one of his marshals with a beautiful baton at a parade. The marshal was extremely proud to receive such a gift from his emperor. But his pride turned to surprise when the baton began to bend! The baton was made of wax. Napoleon was making fun of the marshal, whom he considered to be much too pompous.

152

The Man who did not Exist

According to an entry in the American edition of the biographical directory, *Who's Who*, Aris Rutherford was a whisky consultant. He was born in a whisky distillery, became an expert on the subject and even drank whisky as a hobby. But there was really no such person as Aris Rutherford.

The entry came about when the compilers of *Who's Who* wrote to Rutherford Aris, a well-known chemical engineer, asking him to correct the details about himself for their next edition. They addressed their enquiry, by mistake, to Aris Rutherford. When he received the letter Professor Aris decided to fill in the details in a humorous fashion.

Much to his surprise, the entry was printed exactly as he had written it — even though there was no such person as Aris Rutherford!

Portugal's Master Forger

A rthur Virgilio Alves Reis, an official in Portugal's colonial service, devised one of the most amazingly successful frauds of all time. In 1924 he discovered that the British printers, Waterlow and Sons, had printed some Portuguese bank notes. When he also found out that the Portuguese bank did not check for duplicate notes he put his plan into action.

He sent an associate, Karel Marang, to London to negotiate with the printers. Marang took with him a forged document giving authority for money to be printed using the same plates and the same serial numbers as a previous order, for use in Angola, Africa. Official documents presented to the printers stated this would not cause any confusion in Portugal as the notes were to be overprinted with the name 'Angola' when they reached Africa.

The notes were duly printed and Reis and his accomplices smuggled them into Portugal. For almost a year nothing was suspected but then it was realized that there were a large number of 500-escudo notes in circulation. Investigators were sent to the banks to find out what was happening. When they searched the Bank of Angola and Metropole, which had been set up by Reis, they found packets of the new notes.

Reis was arrested, but because the documents he had forged were so expertly done it was five years before he could be tried. He was eventually sentenced to 20 years in prison. Two of his accomplices also received prison sentences and a third fled the country.

Wet Phones

When people in north London received a telephone call from an engineer saying that there was a fault on the line, they believed him. He said that the fault could only be put right if the receiver was dunked in a bucket of water. Real telephone engineers had quite a job repairing wet telephones.

A Fiver for Free

There in the middle of a pavement in London was a genuine £5 note. Sooner or later someone was bound to notice it and pick it up. But the person who did so was in for a big surprise. The note was glued to the pavement. What the victim did not see was Horace de Vere Cole laughing in the background. In the 1920s Cole was known as the greatest practical joker of all time and this was one of his favourite pranks.

Tickets, Please

As the ticket inspector on the train approached, Edward Nye told his friend, the poet James Whitcomb Riley, to get under the seat as he only had one ticket. Riley was reluctant to follow his friend's request but eventually did so to avoid any trouble.

When the inspector reached him, Nye handed over both tickets. 'Who's the other ticket for?' asked the inspector. Nye pointed to Riley, half hidden beneath the seat. 'It's for my friend. He always travels like that!'

Rare Rabbit

One of the postcards bought by people who visit Yellowstone National Park in Wyoming, USA, shows a rare animal which lives in the region. It is the jackalope, an antlered rabbit that is almost extinct. This rabbit is also unusual because it can imitate human sounds.

If anyone decided to search the plains of Wyoming for this rare creature they would be disappointed. It does not exist. But many people who see the postcard believe the photograph to be quite genuine.

Putting Couani on the Map

During the autumn of 1902, the President of Couani called a Press conference at his luxury Paris hotel. Some of the reporters had never heard of Couani and according to the President, Adolphe Brezet, that was the reason for the Press conference. Brezet explained that Couani had long been under the dominance of its powerful neighbour, Brazil, but as it had now gained its independence he had been sent to Paris to inform the world of its existence.

The President spoke so convincingly of his country, that the reporters believed him, and by the end of the year everyone in Paris had heard of Couani.

Early in 1903, the first Couani embassy opened in Paris and this was soon followed by consulates in London, Rome, Berlin and Madrid.

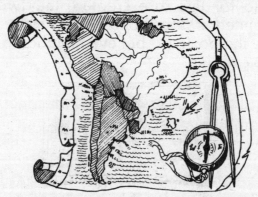

In 1904, Brezet had letters from both the Japanese and Russian governments. The two nations were at war and urgently needed more ships. Would it be possible, both nations wondered, for the famous Couani shipyards to build them? Somewhat unusually, Brezet took a while to reply. Meanwhile, the two countries checked up on Couani with their ambassadors in Brazil. Much to their surprise, they were informed that there was no such place.

Making an Ass of the Art World

Paintings by Raphael Boronali were greeted by the art world as masterpieces when they first appeared in Paris in 1977. The paintings turned out to have been 'painted' by a donkey with a paintbrush attached to its tail!

UFO Photo

In 1962, an English schoolboy called Alex Birch amazed the scientific world with a photograph of a UFO (unidentified flying object). It was accepted as genuine and published all over the world. Birch became a celebrity and was interviewed several times on television and on radio. He was even quizzed for three hours by government experts in Whitehall.

Ten years later, Birch admitted that the photograph was a fake. It was a hoax that had got out of hand. He had taken the picture as a joke for his school magazine, but things had happened so fast that he couldn't admit the truth.

Stop Thief!

A policeman was walking through Central Park in New York when he saw a man running off with one of the park benches. He caught him and arrested him but the man then produced a receipt for the bench. It belonged to

him! The man was arch joker, Hugh Troy, and he had bought the bench a short while earlier with the sole intention of hoaxing a policeman.

Laugh in Leeds

Many listeners to Radio Leeds in England were furious when they heard that their city square was to be demolished and that the statue of the Black Prince was to be sold. Some were consoled, however, by the news that local citizens would be able to buy cheap petrol from Arab sources in return for the statue.

Whatever their views, listeners realized how gullible they were when they discovered the story to be an April Fool joke.

Haggis Hoax

I n 1973, listeners to the British Radio Four programme, *Sunday*, were intrigued by a report from broadcaster, Ted Harrison. He was at a Scottish monastery which was famous for the production of Scotland's national delicacy, the haggis. These monks apparently made the dish from an ancient and very secret recipe. It was, of course, a hoax.

Silent Speech

F ilm pioneer, Jesse Lasky, was very proud of his ability to deliver a good speech at a moment's notice. One day, he accepted an invitation from cinema owner, Sid Grauman, to talk to a group of film distributors about the state of the industry.

When he walked on to the floodlit stage, he was rather disappointed at the lack of applause. He started with a witty introduction designed to make the audience laugh, but they made no sound to show their appreciation.

Undeterred, Lasky continued with his hour-long speech but it was hard going for he received absolutely no reaction from the audience. At the end of the speech there was no applause. Then the lights went up and Lasky discovered that the whole audience consisted of wax dummies!

Caravan Caper

Film producer, Mel Brooks, was delighted when actor, Frank Sinatra, allowed him to borrow his studio caravan to entertain a friend. Brooks was new to Hollywood and was extremely grateful that the star had been kind enough to offer his help.

After a few drinks, Brooks and his friend felt they needed a breath of fresh air so they went out of the caravan for a walk. When they stepped outside they were astonished to find that they did not know where they were. Frank Sinatra had hired a truck to take the caravan to a side street several miles away. It was some time before Mel Brooks found his way back to the studio!

Phone Fault

The telephone caller said he was a telephone engineer. 'There's a rather serious fault,' he said. 'Your line is blocking all the other telephones in the area. Could you please cut the cord and that will free the congestion. There will be a telephone engineer at your house in 20 minutes to mend your phone.'

Somewhat surprisingly, many people in Lancashire, England, who received that call believed it to be genuine and dutifully cut the telephone cord as told. Real telephone engineers were not too pleased when they heard of the hoax. They had quite a few telephones to repair.

Vote for Yetta

Mrs Yetta Bronstein was one of the candidates in the 1964 American Presidential campaign. Her slogan was 'Vote for Yetta and things will get Better'. Yetta Bronstein was a middle-aged housewife from the Bronx area of

New York. She felt that the country needed a mother-figure and it seemed a lot of ordinary voters agreed with her; 'I'm voting for Yetta' badges were worn by people all over the city.

No one seemed to wonder why Yetta Bronstein was never seen in public or why there were no photographs of her. The reason was simple — she did not exist! She had been invented by Alan Abel, a well-known hoaxer, and his wife.

The Green Cliffs of Dover

Listeners to BBC Radio Four's *Today* programme were once told, on 1 April, that fast-breeding algae were turning the white cliffs of Dover green. Many listeners believed it.

My Word is My Bond

When the wealthy Austrian count came to visit Mr Green's farm, the two immediately struck a deal. Green wanted to sell his run-down farm and the Austrian seemed willing to pay over the odds for it. It transpired that the count had sold his family jewels and now had $50 000 in bonds. (These are certificates issued by a company or government that prove that the holder will be paid the specified sum of money on a certain date.) The count offered $25 000 in bonds for the farm, and Green readily agreed; the farm was worth a lot less than that.

'To get the farm up to standard I shall need some working capital,' said the count. 'Do you know of anyone who could change some of my remaining bonds for me?' Green was also a banker and was very pleased to cash $25 000 of the bonds for the count.

Later that evening the two men, and another banker, met in the count's hotel room. Mr Green handed over $25 000 and the deeds for the farm in exchange for $50 000 in bonds. To seal the deal in traditional Austrian manner the count insisted that they drink to it.

By the end of the evening, the two bankers were feeling the effects of the drink and did not bother to check the bonds very carefully. When they did so the following day they discovered that all they had was a pile of worthless newspaper. They had been duped by 'Count' Victor Lustig, one of the greatest confidence tricksters the world has ever known.

The Two-wheel Car

It sounded like a major breakthrough in car production – a two-wheeled car that combined the five-seat comfort of a saloon car with the speed and fuel economy of a motor-cycle. There was just one snag. The vehicle had a tendency to fall over when it came to a stop. This problem was solved by fitting bulldozer-style wide tyres and a computer-linked gyroscope.

According to the report which appeared in the British newspaper, the *Daily Mail*, in 1983, the car was expected to be in production within a few years. Only one more problem had to be solved – the fact that the vehicle had to be propped up when parked.

Later the newspaper suggested that the story be taken with a pinch of salt!

Fair Cops

Prior to his marriage to Sarah Ferguson in July, 1986, Prince Andrew held a party for some of his friends. Towards the end of the evening three policewomen entered the club, stayed for a short while and then left. It turned out that they were Pamela Stevenson, the Princess of Wales and Sarah Ferguson!

What's been Stolen?

Hugh Troy, one of America's most talked of practical jokers, once left a pile of burglary equipment outside the Metropolitan Museum of Art in New York, USA. This caused a stir among the museum staff. They organized a frantic search of the premises to see which of their treasures had been stolen during the night.

Prove You are Guilty

Hans van Meegeren was arrested in July, 1945, for selling a painting to the Nazi leader, Hermann Goering, during the Second World War. This was considered to be collaborating with the Germans, the punishment for which was death. The painting was *The Women Taken in Adultery* by the Dutch master, Vermeer.

In court, Meegeren insisted that he had not collaborated. The 'Vermeer' was a forgery that he had painted himself. The judge was naturally reluctant to believe him but he gave Meegeren the chance to paint another 'Vermeer' that would fool the experts. So, under supervision, Meegeren painted a new 'Vermeer' which he called *Jesus Among the Doctors*. The painting was good enough to convince the court, and the collaboration charges were dropped.

Several other paintings, supposedly by Vermeer, were then discovered to be Meegeren's. He was brought to trial again, this time charged with deception. Meegeren was given a prison sentence of one year but he died of a heart attack six weeks later – aged 57.

Charlie's Surprise

The great film comedian, Charlie Chaplin, once entered a Charlie Chaplin Look-Alike Contest for a laugh. To his surprise, he didn't win.

Pyjama Game

Heart-throb film star Rudolph Valentino apologized to the audience at a film première for appearing in his pyjamas; he had overslept. And then to everyone's surprise he began to remove his pyjamas. The audience gasped, but apprehension soon gave way to laughter. Valentino was wearing a suit underneath his pyjamas.

A Boost for the Museum

I n 1960, the directors of the Gothenburg Museum in Sweden were looking for a way to attract more visitors to their displays. They decided to exhibit a strange creature called a *Vitrysk Strandmuddlare* (a white Russian shore-muddler).

The white Russian shore-muddler is a very strange creature indeed. Its head and fore-parts are from a baby wild pig, its tusks are made from the teeth of an alligator, its hind-quarters and tail are those of a squirrel and its back feet are those of a water fowl. It is such a deliberate hoax that it is unlikely that anyone would be fooled into believing it to be real. But just in case anyone should be deceived, the museum displays the creature only once a year — on 1 April.

The American Rhinoceros

O n a snowy day at Cornell University, in Ithaca, New York State, Hugh Troy borrowed a friend's wastepaper basket made from the foot of a rhinoceros. He tied some lengths of rope to it and then, with the help of a colleague, swung the foot to and fro so that it left footprints

in the snow. Keeping some distance away from the prints they were making, the two men walked through the university campus.

The next day, the footprints were identified by a zoologist as those of a rhinoceros and the event caused quite a stir — especially as the prints ended in the middle of a frozen lake in the centre of which was an enormous hole!

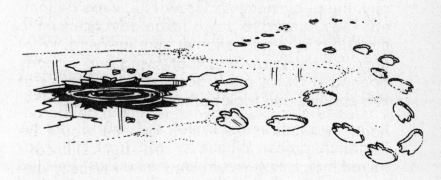

The Mystery of Dr James Barry

In 1809, James Barry entered Edinburgh University as a medical student. Two years later, at the age of 12 he qualified as a doctor. At the age of 17 he became an army surgeon. He pursued a brilliant medical career in Cape Town and all over the world, finally returning to Britain in 1864. The following year he died and for the first time his secret was revealed. He was a woman!

Hughes Hoax

Howard Hughes was an eccentric American millionaire who lived the life of a recluse and was never seen in public. When Clifford Irving approached a publishing house and pretended that Hughes had given him permission to 'ghost' (co-write) his autobiography, the publishers, McGraw-Hill, were delighted. They agreed to pay a large advance sum to the millionaire and another sum to Irving. What they did not know was that Irving had already opened a Swiss bank account in the name of H R Hughes and took both sums himself.

Irving was able to travel the world on his ill-gotten gains. Whenever McGraw-Hill contacted him, Irving would say he had just finished another interview with the millionaire and that the book was coming along fine.

Unfortunately for Irving, another hoaxer came up with the same idea and made a similar offer to a different publisher who immediately announced the fact. Naturally, McGraw-Hill instantly made it known that they had already negotiated exclusive rights with the millionaire. The news got back to Hughes, himself, and a private detective was hired to investigate. It was not long before Irving's fraud was discovered.

The Three-humped Camel

An advertisement once appeared in a Welsh local paper which read: 'Lost — one three-humped camel. Owner desperate. Reward.' A telephone number was given for people to ring.

The landlord of the local pub was not very pleased. It was his number that had been given and over 70 people rang him, claiming to have seen his non-existent camel.

Cat Catch

One of the exhibits on show at one of P T Barnum's shows was the Cherry-Coloured Cat. When visitors had paid their money they were shown an ordinary black cat. Well, some cherries are black!

An Unfair Cop

In 1976, motorists in Maidstone, Kent, in England, began receiving parking tickets for no reason whatsoever, and the local traffic wardens were blamed for being too keen. Then some drivers looked at the tickets in more detail and were rather shocked. The writing on the tickets was extremely rude! A police officer in charge of the town's traffic wardens explained that the tickets were a hoax. 'We want to make it clear that we are not responsible for the fakes,' he said. 'We wish we knew who it was.'

Multiple Monas

On 21 August, 1911, one of the world's most famous paintings, the *Mona Lisa*, was stolen from the Louvre in Paris. In the following six months at least six wealthy Americans bought what they thought to be the genuine *Mona Lisa*. But they were all fakes, painted by master forger, Yves Chaudron. But the frauds did not make Chaudron any wealthier. All the money he made was stolen by one of his accomplices.

The Cardiff Giant

S tubby Newell had hired two men to dig a well at his farm near Cardiff, New York, USA. They were rather surprised when they hit something solid about 1 metre (3 feet) underground. They cleared away the earth and to their amazement discovered the fossilized body of a giant man.

News soon got around about the incredible find and so many people wanted to see it that Stubby erected a tent over the site and charged visitors 50 cents to look at the giant. Some maintained that it was an ancient statue but others believed it to be the fossil remains of a giant human.

Eventually, the Cardiff Giant was exhibited in the nearby town of Syracuse. Then the great showman, P T Barnum, never one to miss out on a money-making idea, commissioned some sculptors to carve a similar giant for his show. He called it 'The Original Cardiff Giant'. Both giants continued to draw the crowds.

Barnum's giant was a fake — but what of the man found in Stubby Newell's field? Well, as was later discovered, that was a fake as well. It had been commissioned a year and a half previously by George Hull, Stubby's cousin. Hull got the idea after hearing a preacher talk about the giants mentioned in Genesis in the Old Testament. The giant had been stained with sulphuric acid to make it look old and buried for a year to add the finishing touches.

George Washington's Nurse

In 1835, P T Barnum made a great deal of money by exhibiting an old lady called Joice Heth. She was said to be 161 years old and had been the nurse to George Washington, the first President of America. In 1836, Joice Heth died and it was revealed that she was in fact about 80 years old. The public complained it had been duped but Barnum insisted that he had hired the old lady believing her story to be true. A case of the hoaxer being hoaxed?

179

Magnetic Money

An American con-man once fiddled a great deal of money from a bank, by means of a surprisingly simple trick. He opened an account at the bank and was given a supply of paying-in slips. These were printed with his account number in magnetic ink. Knowing that the computer picked up magnetic ink and not ordinary ink, the man simply went to the bank, removed the loose slips left on the counter for the use of customers, and substituted the slips bearing his account number. No matter what account number was written on the slip, the computer picked up his number printed in magnetic ink. After three days the con-man closed his account and got away with $100 000!

On The Wrong Side

An April Fool item on Paris radio once caused traffic chaos in the French capital. It was announced that from 1 April all Europe would drive on the left.

The result was absolute pandemonium: drivers who had heard the broadcast drove on the left of the road, while those who had not listened in stayed on the right.

Washing the White Lions

On 1 April, 1860, several people in London received invitations to the Tower of London. They were asked to gather at the White Gate to witness the annual ceremony of washing the white lions. There was confusion when the guests reached the Tower. The gate proved to be as non-existent as the event.

The Isles of San Serriffe

I n 1977, the British newspaper, *The Guardian* published a report about the semi-colon-shaped Isles of San Serriffe which were celebrating their 10th year of independence. The report contained several advertisements and an interview with the islands' president, General Maria-Jesu Pica. There was also a competition in which readers could win two weeks' holiday in the islands.

Very few people realized that the name of the republic and its president were derived from printing terms. And, somewhat surprisingly, only one person complained about the hoax. The closing date for entries for the competition was 31 March — the day before the item was published, on 1 April!

Sentences from the Sentenced

When an advertisement appeared in several European magazines that some Italian girls were looking for male pen friends, many men replied. Several of them built up a regular correspondence and eventually arranged a meeting. Each one followed the same pattern. The girl would write to say that she did not have enough money for the journey. Quite naturally the man, who by then thought he had a good chance of marrying the girl, would send her the fare. But when the man went to the meeting place the girl did not turn up.

One man decided to investigate further and visit the girl in her own home. When he got there he found it was a jail! The young Italian girls were in fact five male prisoners and they made quite a bit of money from their scheme.

The Six-horse Race

Arthur Bottomley, an English confidence trickster, once devised what appeared to be a foolproof way of winning a lot of money on horse racing.

He made sure that he owned all the horses in a race in Blankenburg, Belgium, but pretended that they were all owned by different people. The jockeys were told in which order they were to finish and he hired several people to place bets on his behalf.

The scheme seemed perfect, but once the race had started, a thick mist blew in from the sea. The jockeys lost sight of each other in the fog and eventually crossed the finishing line in the wrong order.

Come to the Party

Film director, Robert Altman, wondered what on earth had happened when hordes of people turned up at his home for a party. The guests had all received invitations, but Altman knew nothing about the party.

A short while later he was inundated with people who wanted to be extras on his next film. It had been announced on a local television station that he was looking for 2500 extras.

Then he found out who was behind the hoax. It was actor, Paul Newman. When the two men had worked together on the film, *Buffalo Bill and the Indians*, Altman had filled Newman's on-location caravan with popcorn, for a joke. To get his own back, Paul Newman had arranged the invitations and television announcement.

Let Us Spray

The men in white coats apologized for causing a bit of a traffic jam but explained to the waiting motorists that their tyres had to be sprayed to prevent the spread of a mysterious plague that was wiping out wildlife in the area. Most motorists accepted the story without question. A few complained and police then discovered that the 'scientists' were students from a university who had thought up the hoax.

A Cheep Trick

During the Second World War, the British Prime Minister, Winston Churchill, often had meetings with President Roosevelt of USA. The two men occasionally had breakfast together whilst discussing world affairs. On one such occasion, Churchill received quite a surprise. He cracked open his boiled egg – and a live chick popped out!

Churchill had fallen prey to Roosevelt's favourite joke. Before breakfast he had put the chick into an empty shell, made some pin holes in part of the shell so the chick could breathe and then sealed the two halves together.

Soldier of Fortune

I n 1918, the Metropolitan Museum of Art in New York paid $40 000 for a large statue of an Etruscan warrior. It had been made in the 5th century — or so the museum believed. In 1960, the statue and several other items purchased over the intervening years were proved to be fakes. They had been made by three Italian sculptors who had managed to earn a great deal of money from the gullible museum authorities.

Skullduggery

In 1912, Charles Dawson, an amateur geologist, was searching for specimens in a gravel pit on Piltdown Common in Sussex. He discovered flint tools, fossilized teeth and then parts of a human skull. Later it was estimated that the skull was 500 000 years old.

It was a great find for Dawson — but even greater treasures were in store. Later, with his friend Dr Arthur Smith Woodward, he found part of a jaw. As this was unearthed near to the original find it was assumed that it came from the same person. But this could have been no ordinary person; it had the jaw of an ape. And yet the teeth had been ground down not as an ape's, but as human teeth are worn away. It seemed that here at last was the proof that Man was descended from ape-like creatures. The skull and the jaw provided evidence of the so-called missing link — the link between Man and the apes.

The remains were displayed in the Natural History Museum in London and 'Piltdown Man', as the exhibit was known, became famous throughout the world.

After a while, Piltdown Man began to arouse suspicion. Evidence arising from other discoveries did not fit in with the ape man. By 1953, there was so much controversy surrounding it that a more detailed examination of the remains was carried out.

As a result of this examination, an official announcement was made, on 21 November, 1953, which declared Piltdown Man to be a fraud. It was disclosed that some of the tools found at the site had been aged artificially, and that the jaw of Piltdown Man had actually belonged to an orang-utan. Even the skull was not as old as had first been thought.

But one mystery still remains. It has never been proved who devised the fraud or why.

The Bare-fronted Hoodwink

I n the Royal Scottish Museum in Edinburgh there is a strange looking bird. It has a large black head, brown wings and a white breast with a large patch of bright red.

The bird was first shown on 1 April, 1975, and the date gives a clue to its origins. It is an April Fool hoax. It was in fact made by Willie Sterling, a taxidermist at the museum. He named the bird 'the bare-fronted hoodwink'.

Cadillac Crash

A n insurance salesman had been pestering the staff of a local radio station in Chicago, USA, to take out insurance with him. They had managed to put up with his continual calls and visits but when he began to use their telephones for personal calls, they decided they had had enough.

While he was using one of the radio station's telephones, one of the staff called him, pretending to be a wealthy tycoon. 'I'm speaking from my new Cadillac,' said the fake businessman. 'I have just bought the car and I want fully-comprehensive insurance immediately.' 'You've got it,' said the excited insurance man. 'You are covered as from this minute. We can sort out the details later.'

At that point, one of the radio engineers switched on a tape recording of a terrifying car crash, and then the phone went dead. The insurance man spent an hour phoning the police and hospitals trying to find out what had happened. He eventually realized that he had been hoaxed by the staff of the radio station and never pestered them again.

A Fortune Down Under

Katherine Riach and her husband, Tom, were absolutely delighted when they received a telephone call to say that they had inherited a fortune in Australia from a rich relative there. Tom decided to give up his job in a brewery in Newcastle, England, and start a new life of luxury down under.

It was some time before the Riachs realized that they had no relatives in Australia and that they had been hoaxed.

Upside-down Room

Rudolph Schenk was a rich American who loved to play jokes on people. He would often invite people to visit his luxurious home where he would treat them to a hearty meal and rather too much to drink. The guest would then be invited to stay the night to sleep off the effects of the alcohol.

When the guest was sound asleep Schenk had him transferred to a specially-built room. The floor of the room was painted white, like a ceiling, and a chandelier rose up from it. The real ceiling was painted to look like floorboards and furniture was fixed to it. There were no windows in the room but Schenk had a secret spy hole through which he could watch what happened when the guest woke up to find himself in an upside-down room.

How to Defy Gravity

Patrick Moore is a respected astronomer with a great reputation as an expert in his field. One morning in 1976 he explained on a BBC radio programme that the gravitational pull on the Earth would be decreased by the fact that the planet Pluto was passing close to Jupiter. To test it, he told people to jump into the air at exactly 9.47 that morning. They would feel lighter and would be able to float in the air for several seconds.

It seems that lots of people believed him as they telephoned the BBC to say that the experiment had worked. They must have been very gullible, particularly as the date was 1 April.

The Winged Sea-dragon

In 1749, fishermen off the coast of Suffolk, England, found a strange animal in their mackerel nets. When it was eventually captured it was seen to be a small winged sea-dragon. Its body was covered in scales, rather like those of an alligator and it had very sharp teeth. It also had wings so it was able to swim and fly.

The sea-dragon was a hoax and had in fact been made from the skin of an angel shark moulded into the shape of a small dragon.

Footprints on the Ceiling

A man was visiting his friend, the great American president, Abraham Lincoln. He walked into one room and received quite a surprise. Someone had walked across the ceiling! Up the walls and across the ceiling there was a track of clear footprints.

194

Later he discovered that Lincoln was the man behind the hoax. It was one of his favourite jokes. He would have a room painted and then hold someone upside down to 'walk' across the ceiling, leaving footprints in the paint.

Shoe Inspection

In 1971 it was announced over the public address system at the Royal Air Force base at Cranwell, England, that a fault had been discovered in all shoes issued to officers. The owners were asked to hand their shoes in at the porter's lodge for checking. A great many officers did so, but those that had recognized the voice knew better. It had been Prince Charles, who had a reputation for pulling practical jokes.

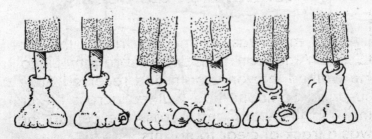

Air Shortage

Overweight Americans were alarmed when it was announced that anyone weighing over 89 kilograms (14 stone) was to be deported. This drastic measure had become necessary, the newspaper reports said, because pollution was leading to a shortage of oxygen. As fat people consumed more than their fair share of air, they had to go.

People realized that the proposal was a hoax when they discovered that the reports had been written by Alan Abel, a New Yorker who was well known for his amazing and successful practical jokes.

Stone's Stories

Louis T Stone of Winsted, Connecticut, USA, was a reporter with an unusual flair. He did not report stories — he made them up. Many of the newspaper editors who used his material between 1895 and 1933 knew the stories were hoaxes — but they were so popular they continued to use them.

Among Stone's stories were those of the bald man who was pestered by flies — so he painted a spider on his head to keep them away; a chicken farmer who plucked his chickens with a vacuum cleaner; and a cat with a harelip that could whistle *Yankee Doodle Dandy*.

Stone made Winsted so famous that a sign was put up at the edge of the town: 'Winsted, Connecticut, founded in 1779, has been put on the map by the ingenious and queer stories that emanate from this town and which are printed all over the country, thanks to L T Stone.'

What's in the Tin?

When Mary Windsor opened a tin of steak for lunch, she found peas! Luckily she had some other tins of meat so she opened another one — it was full of pears! She opened several other tins of steak, but they all contained different things.

Eventually she became so frustrated that she complained to the local grocer, only to find that he had received similar complaints from other customers. He was most apologetic and had no idea what could have happened. If he had glanced at the grinning face of Mary's husband, actor, Frank Windsor, he might have guessed. When no one was looking he had removed the labels from the steak tins and stuck them on to other tins. The mix up caused confusion for several months.

Commercial Con

T here was a lot of excitement in a small English village when a television crew began setting up its equipment on the green. The television people were there to film a commercial for a certain brand of baked beans.

Seventy local housewives were recruited by the producer to sing the praises of the beans. For 10 minutes they sang at the tops of their voices as they marched through the village towards the green – just as the television people had directed them to do.

When they marched on to the village green, the housewives realized they had been hoaxed. There was not a television camera in sight – the 'television crew' had gone.

Police Sale

According to the official-looking poster, the police at Bath, England, were going to have a sale of unclaimed lost property and stolen goods. Bargains included radios at 50p each and a Ferrari car for £3000. The police were not very pleased – they knew nothing about the bargain sale.

Fooling the President

Lyndon Johnson, President of the USA, 1963-69, once visited an air base to improve the morale of troops being sent to fight in Vietnam. But the morale of the troops he was due to meet was so low that they had drunk too much and were not in a fit state to be seen.

The solution arrived at was to allow the President to meet troops who had just *returned* from Vietnam. Johnson was so impressed by the laughing and joking and, thinking that they were

about to leave, he insisted on waving goodbye to them. The men had to get back on to the plane from which they had just disembarked and perform a fake departure. The aircraft then flew around the base until the President had left.

An Amusing Feet

When Hugh Troy, the American prankster, was at Cornell University, in Ithaca, New York State, he played a joke on one of his professors. He painted human feet on the toe cap of the professor's boots, then painted over them with soluble black paint so the boots appeared normal. When the professor walked out in the rain the black paint dissolved, leaving him apparently walking about in his bare feet!

Cure for the Common Cold

S cientists have been searching for a cure for the common cold for a long time. The breakthrough came in 1973 when a Dr Clothier announced on British Radio that it had been discovered that Dutch elm disease cured the common cold. There appeared to be some unusual side effects to the cure, however. One scientist, after treating himself with powdered Dutch elm, had actually caught Dutch elm disease himself. As a result, his red hair had turned yellow and he had eventually become bald. Dr Clothier therefore warned all red-haired listeners to avoid any areas where Dutch elm disease was present.

One wonders how many listeners took the scientific talk seriously and how many actually realized that Dr Clothier was, in reality, comedian, Spike Milligan.

The Space Age Revette

N ew cars are produced every year but the three-wheeled Revette, launched in America in 1974, seemed to be well in advance of its time. Its space age design and revolutionary new engine, providing a remarkable fuel consumption attracted much attention.

The owner of the company persuaded people to invest in the company to enable it to start production. But when the car appeared for its first demonstration the engine only ran for a second or two and then refused to restart.

The company moved to a new factory in Texas where the police began to take an interest in its activities. They decided to take a look inside the factory. All they found inside was a pile of rubbish, bits from a Datsun, a Volkswagen and an old lawnmower.

Investing in the Theatre

A wealthy theatre producer in the USA was planning a musical. A businessman approached the producer and persuaded him to talk about the production. It sounded magnificent but would cost $70 000 to put on. The producer himself only had $36 000 so the businessman insisted that he be allowed to put up the rest.

What the businessman did not realize was that he was dealing with 'Count' Victor Lustig, the undoubted king of the confidence tricksters during the 1920s.

Later that day, they met in Lustig's hotel room. Lustig produced his $36 000 (in forged notes) and the businessman added his money to the pile. The money was locked safely away and the two men went out for a drink to discuss the plans for the musical.

In the middle of the meeting, a porter arrived from the hotel to say that Lustig had to telephone New York urgently. Lustig said he would be right back and left. The businessman never saw him or his money again.

Where there's a Will

Douglas Fairbanks, the film star, promised four close friends that they would receive something in his will when he died. But when the will was read after Fairbanks's death in 1939 there was no mention in it of anything left to his friends.

Two months later, Douglas Fairbanks Jnr asked the four to come and see him. He gave each of them an envelope containing a cheque for $60 000. His father had left the four out of his will – just for a laugh.

205

Computerized Crime

A computer expert in an American bank recently devised a fraud that would make him a lot of money. He ordered the computer to take just 10 cents from each customer's account and to transfer it to the last account on the record. He then opened an account with a surname starting with the letter Z. It worked well until a Mr Zydel opened an account. Mr Zydel could not understand why his bank balance kept increasing so he queried the matter and the employee's fraud was exposed.

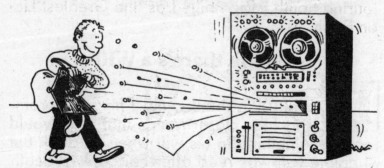

The Greatest Liar on Earth

In an article in the magazine, *Wide World*, published in 1898, Louis de Rougement described how he had spent 30 years living with cannibals in north-western Australia after he had been shipwrecked.

He told how he had participated in cannibal feasts and how he had built himself a house of pearl shells. He also described how he had cured himself of fever by sleeping inside a dead buffalo and claimed to have ridden on the backs of 270-kilogram (600-pound) turtles.

He became an instant celebrity and received numerous invitations to talk to scientific societies about his adventures. So famous were his exploits that a model of him was placed in Madame Tussaud's, the famous waxwork gallery in London. When he was eventually exposed as a fraud he made the most of the situation by touring South Africa billed as 'the Greatest Liar on Earth'.

Miss Radio One

|S| imon Bates was the reporter for the Miss Radio One Beauty Contest in 1977, in Britain. The winner must have been quite something for she came from an uninhabited island off the coast of Scotland and was described as wearing a three-piece bathing costume! Of course this was a hoax, as a beauty contest could not possibly take place on the radio.

The Tichborne Claimant

|S| ir Roger Tichborne, heir to the Tichborne estates in Hampshire, England, disappeared at sea in 1854. His mother received no news from him but refused to believe he was dead. Eleven years later she advertised in newspapers in South America and Australia offering a reward for information about her son.

The advertisement was seen in Australia by a petty criminal, Arthur Orton, who wrote to the old lady claiming he was her long-lost son. In 1866, Orton sailed for England. He went to Hampshire and found out as much as he could about the family before visiting Lady Tichborne.

Orton bore no resemblance to the missing heir. At the time of his disappearance, Tichborne had weighed 57 kilograms (9 stone), had straight dark hair, and a tattoo on his left arm. He also spoke fluent French. Orton weighed 152.5 kilograms (24 stone), had wavy hair, no tattoo and could not speak French. But somehow Orton succeeded in deceiving the old lady.

When Lady Tichborne died, Orton took his claim to court where his impersonation was not so successful. He was arrested, charged with perjury and brought to trial. On 1 March, 1874, he was sentenced to 14 years in prison.

Chinese Tricks

When the great Chinese magician, Chung Ling Soo, died on the stage of the Wood Green Empire, London, in 1918, his greatest trick was revealed. For many years he had fooled the British public into believing he was genuinely Chinese — he even spoke through interpreters. The charade was all part of a gigantic hoax. He was an American, without a trace of Chinese blood, called William Ellsworth Robinson.

A Shaggy-dog Story

A large number of talented animals have been featured on Esther Rantzen's television programme *That's Life*. Possibly the most remarkable was a sheepdog called Tramp. Tramp was so clever he could even drive a car.

The programme showed Tramp at the wheel of a specially-converted Mini and he certainly was a very competent driver. Many viewers thought it was rather dangerous to let a dog drive a car and hundreds telephoned to complain. What they did not realize was that Tramp was really a woman dressed in a sheepdog costume.

Spaghetti Harvest

On 1 April, 1957, a film about the Swiss spaghetti harvest was shown on British television, with a commentary by Richard Dimbleby, one of the country's most respected presenters. Swiss peasants were shown gathering spaghetti from the trees in the Ticino district and Richard Dimbleby gave a serious explanation of how spring had come early that year, producing a bumper spaghetti harvest.

Hundreds of people telephoned the BBC after the programme. There were no complaints that they had been hoaxed — all they wanted to know was where they could buy spaghetti plants. In answer to this question they were told that such plants were not available in Britain but that some British enthusiasts had produced some acceptable results by planting a small tin of spaghetti in tomato sauce!

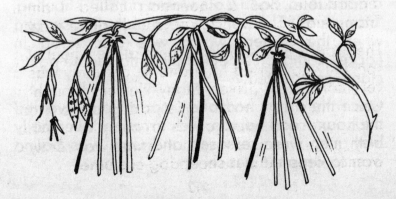

An Arresting Prank

The British politician, Oliver Locker-Lampson, once announced that it was unthinkable that a Member of Parliament would ever be arrested. But he reckoned without the wiles of Horace de Vere Cole, a brilliant practical joker who was quick to prove him wrong.

Cole challenged the politician to a race along a London street, which Locker-Lampson accepted. As he explained the rules of the race, Cole secretly slipped his watch into the MP's pocket.

Then they were off, and Locker-Lampson built up a good lead. Soon Cole was in pursuit, shouting, 'Stop, thief!' The police joined in the chase, and when the 'stolen' watch was discovered in Locker-Lampson's pocket the unfortunate politician was arrested.

Once the arrest had been made Cole revealed the hoax – and he, too, was arrested! Eventually both men were released and Cole was bound over to keep the peace.

Caught by Crooked Crooks

In 1976, several federal agents in the USA posed as crooks and let it be known that they were fences (people who buy stolen goods from criminals). They bought everything offered to them and, as a result, recovered millions of dollars worth of stolen property and made more than 200 arrests.

A Move for St Paul's

On 1 April, 1982, a British television announcer on ITN's *News at One* announced that St Paul's Cathedral in London was to be moved to London's Isle of Dogs — brick by brick. To most people it sounded like a really crazy idea — and that is what it was. The story was a hoax.

The Bionic Horse

In 1977, on the eve of the famous British horse race, the Grand National, a reporter from Radio Merseyside interviewed the owner of a bionic horse that had been entered for the race. The horse was said to have had a plastic bone implanted in one of its hind legs which helped it to bounce over the fences. Listeners thought it was bound to win – until they realized that the eve of the Grand National was 1 April.

Order of the Bath

During the First World War the writer H L Mencken, wrote a joke article on the history of the bathtub in America. Entitled 'A Neglected Anniversary', it appeared in the *New York Evening Mail* on 28 December, 1917.

Much to Mencken's surprise the article was accepted as a genuine piece, and it was not long before the 'facts' he had invented for a laugh were being quoted by other people in serious articles about bathing.

Several years later, Mencken thought that the hoax had gone far enough. He wrote a feature pointing out that he had made up the history but that the joke had now got out of hand. This article appeared in several American newspapers on 23 May, 1926, but in spite of it, Mencken's invented facts continued to be quoted for over 35 years.

Unique Gruck

T he Royal Scottish Museum in Edinburgh owns the only known specimen of a gruck – a bird that has the body of a red grouse and the head of a tufted duck. It is the only one in existence because it was made by Ian Lyster, the museum's taxidermist.

Monuments for Sale

I t was a sunny day in the 1920s. While strolling through London's Trafalgar Square, Arthur Furguson spotted an American tourist admiring Nelson's Column and offered to be his guide. He told the American about the statue and the great naval hero to whom it was dedicated. When the American let it slip that he was wealthy, Furguson told him that Britain was being forced to sell the statue to pay off some of its debts.

'How much will Britain want for it?' inquired the American. 'A mere £6000,' sighed Furguson, 'but we will only sell it to someone who appreciates its place in our history and who is prepared to look after it.' The American fell for Furguson's story and decided to purchase the monument himself. By the time he realized he had been conned, Furguson had cashed the cheque and disappeared.

Furguson was eventually arrested, but not before he had sold Big Ben to another American for £1000, received a down payment of £2000 for Buckingham Palace, leased the White House in Washington DC for $100 000 a year, and almost sold the Statue of Liberty for $100 000 before his hoax was discovered.

Doctor, Doctor

Doctor Joseph C Cyr was one of the best medical officers to serve on board the Canadian ship *Cayuga*. So good was he, that the Canadian Navy's public relations officer in the Far East prepared a Press release describing the young doctor's skill and dedication to duty.

Shortly after the story appeared, Commander Plomer and the *Cayuga* received a message to remove Dr Cyr from active duty. It turned out that he was not a doctor at all. The real Dr Cyr had identified him as a man he knew and respected called Dr Cecil B Hamann. But the real Dr Hamann, said the young man was really Ferdinand Waldo Demara who had been expelled from St Louis University in the USA for cheating.

Demara was brought before a naval inquiry board. He was discharged from the service in 1952 and ordered to leave the country.

Wonderful Water

In 1977, thousands of bald-headed men invaded a farm in Rothbury, Northumberland, England, following a spoof television report which claimed that water from the well had amazing hair-restoring properties.

Traffic Ram

A lot of people got into trouble for being late for work when a herd of 500 wild sheep brought the city of Birmingham, in England, to a standstill. Birmingham radio reporter, Mike Henfield, kept listeners informed of the situation and advised them to wait until the area had been cleared before going to work. Many people followed his advice, forgetting that the date was 1 April.

Sound Insult

Filming is not always as glamorous as most people believe. Quite often the actors have to put up with some quite atrocious conditions. Barbara Windsor once discovered this to be true when she was making one of the famous *Carry On* films.

Some of the scenes were shot in an open field in what was supposed to be summer. In fact the field was extremely muddy. During a break between scenes, Barbara moaned about the conditions to co-star Kenneth Williams. She said she would never make another *Carry On* film again and described, in no uncertain terms, exactly what she thought of the producer.

The following day, all the actors went to the viewing room to see the previous day's filming. It proved to be an embarrassing experience for Barbara as all her insults were heard quite clearly. Kenneth Williams had left his microphone on while she had been complaining!

Bogus Doctor

A chauffeur-driven car drew up outside the house of a titled lady in London. From the car, stepped a Harley Street surgeon. He was ushered into the lady's presence and she welcomed him with open arms, thinking that at long last someone would cure her illness.

The doctor gave her some very expensive pills and left the house with £7000 in cash and some valuable jewellery.

Later it turned out that the pills were only pain-killers bought from a local chemist. The 'doctor' was really Stanley Lowe who was known as King of the Con Men.

Early Call

British comedian, Norman Wisdom, was once an Army trumpeter based in India. One evening some of his friends told him that summertime started that night and that he had to put his watch forward by one hour.

Norman assumed that his friends were telling him the truth until he got into trouble the following morning for blowing reveille an hour early and waking the whole regiment.

For Sale – The Eiffel Tower

When he read in a newspaper in March, 1925, that the Eiffel Tower was to be renovated, 'Count' Victor Lustig hit upon the idea for what has since become the most famous fraud of all time. He would sell the Eiffel Tower.

He organized a secret meeting with the heads of several large demolition and salvage companies in Paris. Lustig claimed that the French government secretly planned to demolish the Eiffel Tower, and had appointed him to hire a company to do it. The job of demolition would be offered to the highest bidder who would be allowed to sell the vast quantity of scrap metal obtained, for his company's own profit.

During the meeting Lustig chatted to the bidders, and the next day offered the job to a man called Andre Poisson, but not before he had persuaded Poisson to pay him a large amount of money for arranging the deal in his favour. Poisson was easily bribed and within an hour he had handed Lustig a cheque.

The cheque was quickly cashed and Lustig promptly boarded a train bound for Vienna.

Monty's Double

During the Second World War, Field Marshal Montgomery seemed to have the ability to be in two places at once — and that was in fact the case. Some of Monty's appearances were not him at all but an actor who looked and sounded like him.

The Man who Would be King

Henry VII was crowned King of England after he defeated Richard III at the Battle of Bosworth Field in 1485. Amongst the many people who contested Henry's right to the throne was the ten-year-old Earl of Warwick. Henry dealt with that threat quite simply — he imprisoned the boy in the Tower of London.

A short while later, the Earl miraculously turned up in Ireland where, on 24 May, 1487, he was crowned by the Bishop of Meath as King Edward VI. The newly-crowned king then travelled back

to England to claim his kingdom. With an army of 1500 men he landed on the Lancashire coast and proceeded to march towards London. At Stoke-on-Trent he was stopped by Henry's army and, after a long and bitter battle, Edward's army was defeated and he was taken prisoner.

There were many people who believed the young earl was their rightful king, but Henry knew that his prisoner was an imposter. The real Earl of Warwick had not escaped from the Tower at all. There was only one thing Henry could do to prove that his second prisoner, whose name was Lambert Simnel, was a fraud. He released the real earl from the Tower and showed him to the people.

For pretending to be earl, Simnel could have expected to be put to death. But, to demonstrate how unimportant he considered this upstart, Henry set him to work in the kitchen instead.

Nessie Panic

When a newspaper in Paignton, England, published a photograph taken on a local beach of the Loch Ness Monster, it received several telephone calls from worried readers. But the paper was dated 1 April, 1982, and the story was a joke.

Time in Loo

A notice once appeared on the notice board in a small company. Workers, it said, were spending too long in the lavatory. This was affecting production so it had been decided that, in future, there would be a rota system. Employees whose surname began with the letter A could use the lavatory between 9 a.m. and 9.15 a.m., those whose names began with a B between 9.15 and 9.30 a.m. and so on. Many employees believed the notice to be genuine, but when they complained, the letter was revealed as a hoax.

Man or Ape?

Charles Waterton, squire of Walton Hall, Worcestershire, was a keen traveller and explorer. On one of his visits to South America, in 1828, he came across a strange, human-like animal. It seemed to be a cross between a man and an ape. So intrigued was he that he decided to bring it back to England — but it was so heavy that he had to content himself with just the head.

Known as the Nondescript, it can still be seen today in the City Museum and Art Gallery in Wakefield, England — but it is a fake. Waterton was an expert taxidermist, and he had made the creature himself.

The Most Famous House in London

In 1810, Theodore Hook, a poet from London, bet his friend that he could make an ordinary house the most famous house in London. He chose 54 Berners Street, and his friend took the bet.

A few days later 12 chimney sweeps called at the house, much to the alarm of Mrs Tottingham who lived there. That was just the start. Soon, several coal carts arrived to make a delivery. They were followed by deliveries of furniture, beer and potatoes. Then a hearse arrived, followed by confectioners, wigmakers, hairdressers, doctors – representatives of every trade imaginable. The street was put in chaos and the police arrived on the scene. Then the Duke of York, the Archbishop of Canterbury and several other dignitaries turned up.

Hook had written to all of them, under various pretences, telling them to call at the house. He certainly won his bet. 54 Berners Street became famous overnight.

Multicoloured Radio

T he world is full of modern scientific wonders so it was no surprise to some listeners to Radio Norwich, in England, to hear that their local radio station was experimenting with colour radio. This new system, listeners were warned, would alter the brilliance of tuning lights on their radios.

The experiment proved fairly successful but there were some complaints. One listener complained that colours were flashing from his radio and another moaned that the experiment was affecting traffic lights in his area. This was quite a surprise to the broadcasters for they had transmitted the item as an April Fool joke!

The Height of Deception

Madame Gomez was billed at fairs as 'the tallest woman in the world'. She certainly looked tall but the show was a fraud. Madame Gomez was 1.8 metres (6 foot) tall, but when on show at the fairs she stood on a stool, hidden beneath her long dress, so she appeared to be much taller.

A Question of Mathematics

The great scientist and mathematician, Albert Einstein, visited many universities giving talks on his theory of relativity. One day his chauffeur said, 'Dr Einstein, I've heard you deliver your talk about 30 times. I now know it by heart and I bet I could even give a talk on relativity myself.'

'Well,' said Einstein, 'I'll give you the chance at the next university. They don't know me there so you can give the talk.'

When they reached the university, Einstein pretended to be the chauffeur, and the chauffeur, pretending to be Einstein, gave the talk.

The chauffeur's lecture was word perfect and none of the university professors realized they had been fooled. The ruse was almost discovered, however, when the bogus Einstein was about to leave. One of the professors asked him a very complex question that involved a number of mathematical equations and formulas. The poor man had no idea what the answer was, but he thought quickly. 'The answer to your question is quite simple,' he said. 'In fact it is so easy I'm going to ask my chauffeur to come and answer it for you.'

Turtle Trick

The hotel manager in Paris was pleased when one of the hotel guests, Waldo Peirce, bought her a present. It was a small turtle, and she kept it in her rooms.

She looked after it so well that it grew at a rapid pace. Within a few days it had become enormous. But then a worrying thing happened. The turtle began to get smaller. No matter how much she cared for it, it continued to get smaller and smaller every day.

Then she discovered that Waldo Peirce had tricked her. Each day, he had put a different-sized turtle in the caretaker's quarters. What she had thought was her turtle getting bigger and then smaller was really a series of turtles planted by Peirce.

Measured Mirth

E xcuse me, sir,' said a surveyor to a person in the street, 'I am a surveyor and I wonder if you could please help me by holding this measuring tape for a second or two.'

In most cases the stranger would oblige. And then the surveyor, who was Horace de Vere Cole, an arch-joker during the 1920s would go around the corner to ask another person to hold the other end of the tape. Cole would then retire to a nearby shop doorway and wait, with tears of laughter running down his cheeks, for the moment when his two victims realized that they had been hoaxed.

The Queen's Psychiatrist

B aron David James Rothschild was psychiatrist to Queen Juliana of the Netherlands until 1978. It was then revealed that he was a fraud. In reality he was a Dutch labourer called Henry de Vries.

Dalek DJ

B ritish disc jockey, Jimmy Young, assumed his radio broadcast was proceeding as normal. It was only when people began to telephone the BBC to complain, that he realized something was wrong. Apparently his voice was coming over the air rather like the sound of one of the daleks from *Dr Who*. Fellow radio presenter, Terry Wogan, had arranged for engineers to tamper with Jimmy's microphone.

Prolific Painter

T om Keating was Britain's most prolific art forger. At the end of his life, he himself estimated that there were over 2500 of his forgeries hanging in galleries or on collector's walls, which were still regarded as genuine.

His most famous forgeries were of the 19th-century artist, Samuel Palmer. *Sepham Barn* sold for £9400 as a genuine Palmer, and it was after an expert had written in *The Times* suggesting that this painting was not genuine that the scandal of Keating's fakes broke. The reputations of many people in the art world were ruined as it was discovered how they had been fooled by Keating's paintings.

In 1979, Keating went on trial for forgery at the Old Bailey in London. Charges were dropped, however, when his health deteriorated. Because of his notoriety, his works soon became popular in their own right. He was offered a £25 000 contract from one London gallery and a £30 000 commission for a single portrait, both of which he refused.

Mayoral Arrest

I n 1906, a squad of soldiers were marching through Germany when they were stopped by a captain in the Prussian Guard. The officer ordered the squad's sergeant to carry out an important duty in the name of the emperor. The sergeant had to accompany the officer on a train to the town of Köpenick, taking his squad with him.

At Köpenick they marched into the Town Hall where the bemused and startled mayor was placed under arrest. The captain then marched to the treasurer's office, explained that the mayor was under arrest, and commandeered the town's cashbox. He ordered the sergeant to escort the mayor to Berlin, then he boarded a taxi and left.

The operation was not revealed as a hoax until the mayor and his escort arrived in Berlin. The captain was really a shoemaker called Wilhelm Voigt. Voigt was a petty criminal who had once been imprisoned by the mayor of Köpenick, and had wanted to get his own back.

Millionaire's Prank

The Greek millionaire, Aristotle Onassis, once paid for a whole page in a Paris newspaper to print a hoax report that the Eiffel Tower was to be loaned to Greece.

Invisible Fish

Quite a crowd gathered outside a pet shop in Surrey, England. A notice was advertising some invisible Malayan ghost fish. They peered into the tank in the window, and saw nothing at all. Of course, the tank was empty, but quite a few people went into the shop to ask the price of the non-existent fish.

Votes Galore

In 1928, Charles King was re-elected President of Liberia with a majority of 600 000. His opponent claimed that the vote had been rigged. There were only 15 000 people eligible to vote!

The Abyssinian Visit

Admiral Sir William May, commander-in-chief of the British fleet at Portland was a little annoyed when he received a message from the Foreign Office saying that he had to welcome a party from Abyssinia later in the day. He had other things to do for he had to prepare the fleet for the spring manoeuvres of 1910. But orders are orders and the visit from the Emperor of Abyssinia was obviously important.

Two hours later, the Emperor and his entourage arrived, accompanied by a Foreign Office official, Herbert Cholmondesly. They were duly welcomed on board the flagship HMS *Dreadnought*, shown around the ship and taken below to meet the admiral in his stateroom. Before they left, the visitors were photographed with their navy hosts.

On their return journey to London, the 'Abyssinians' stopped speaking the unintelligible rubbish they had used on board ship and spoke good English. They recalled with glee, the day's events, for the party were not what they seemed. Cholmondesly was in fact a well known practical joker, Horace de Vere Cole, and the Abyssinians were in reality the novelist, Virginia Woolf, sportsman, Anthony Buxton, artist, Duncan Grant, judge's son, Guy Ridley and, accompanying them as an 'interpreter' Virginia Woolf's brother, Adrian.

Feathered Fraud

I n 1879, R Bowdler Sharpe, an authority on birds, described a species of bird that was new to science. He thought it came from Madras and he gave it the Latin name *Lalage melanothorax*. The only real evidence Sharpe had of the bird's existence was a stuffed specimen. Being a scientist of high repute, he examined the specimen several times and even showed it to other scientists. It was not until several years later that he discovered the bird to be a hoax. It had been made from the bodies of two real birds – a drongo and a cuckoo shrike.

Metric Time

B ritain is gradually being converted to metric measurement, so it was no surprise to some people in Birmingham when they received letters stating that the 24-hour clock was to be abolished in favour of a metric system.

Under this new system there would be 10 seconds to the minute, 10 minutes to the hour and 10 hours to the day. Seconds would in future be known as millidays, hours would be decidays, or millimonths, and years would from now on be known as kilodays.

One problem of the new system was that people would have to work longer but would not receive any more money, except in the case of leap kilodays when salaries would be adjusted at the end of the hectoday — every 1.46 decimonths.

As the letter bore the name of the City of Birmingham Education Department, many people believed it to be genuine and several factory managers pinned it to their notice boards. But the letters proved to be an enormous hoax.

Europe's Greatest Imposter

According to his followers, the Count of Cagliostro could turn lead into gold, make diamonds grow larger, convert flax into silk and cure any known ill. For seven years Cagliostro lived in luxury and was the friend of kings, bishops, ministers, scientists, and philosophers. He supplied them with elixirs, prophecies and useful contacts with people in high places. He claimed to have been born before Noah's flood, and to have known Moses and Solomon and been a good friend of Roman emperors. He said he had been instructed in all the sciences by an old sage called Althotas.

In reality, Count Cagliostro had been born in 1743, the son of a poor family in Palermo, Sicily. His name was Guiseppe Balsamo.

During his early life, he stole money from his uncle, forged documents and sold homemade beauty creams. In 1768 he arrived in Rome claiming to be Count Alessandro Cagliostro. He was accompanied by his wife, Lorenza Feliciani, whom he introduced as the Countess Serafina. He claimed to have rescued her from a harem.

The criminal couple travelled all over Europe in princely splendour, but this came to an end when Cagliostro was put into prison for something he

didn't do. While he was in prison his wife began to tell stories of how they had duped everyone in previous years. So when Cagliostro was released, nine months later, people were not so ready to believe his fantastic claims.

Cagliostro was eventually jailed in Italy and he remained in prison until his death in 1795.

Caught by Computer Failure

A man working in a bank in Minnesota, USA programmed its computer to ignore any cheques drawn on his account. The fraud worked quite well – until the computer broke down and his crime was discovered.

Fur-bearing Trout

One day, a lady took a trout covered with white fur to the Royal Scottish Museum in Edinburgh. She had bought the stuffed fish in Canada and wanted to know more about it.

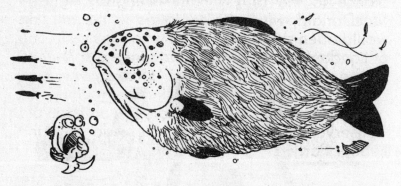

The notice attached to the fish stated that it had been caught in Lake Superior and that it was thought that 'the great depth and the extreme penetrating coldness of the water in which these fish live has caused them to grow their dense coat of (usually) white fur'.

The lady was pleased when the museum told her that the fish was indeed a trout. Then it was explained to her that the fur did not belong to the fish but had in fact come from a rabbit. When she realized that she had been hoaxed, the lady donated the fur-bearing trout to the museum where it remains to this day.

Prime Minister of Mirth

H orace de Vere Cole was well known in London during the 1920s for his hilarious hoaxes; he never missed an opportunity to play a practical joke. Cole bore a striking resemblance to the British Prime Minister, Ramsay MacDonald, which he exploited to the full. He would often stand on a small wooden box in one of London's major streets and make a speech to the passers-by. People were naturally very surprised to see their Prime Minister insulting his own government and persuading people to vote Conservative when he was the leader of the Labour Party.

Radio Sheik Up

The managing director of a radio studio in Liverpool, England, was most impressed when he received a telephone call from a large oil company. When he was told that the sheik, His Eminence Shubtill of Sharjah wanted to visit the studio, he was thrilled.

When the sheik, dressed in a smart suit, white silk head-dress and dark glasses arrived at the studio he was royally entertained. He was also interviewed on the air about oil exploration in the Persian Gulf before being escorted back to his chauffeur-driven white Jaguar.

Later it was discovered that the 'sheik' was really a computer expert called Neville Duncan, who had decided to hoax the radio station because the voice of one of their disc jockeys had been getting on his nerves!

Animals should be Clothed

O n 27 May, 1959, G Clifford Prout, President of the Society Against Indecency of Naked Animals, appeared on American television insisting that all animals should be clothed. He claimed that moral standards in America were declining due to the fact that animals were allowed to go around naked.

The broadcast was an immediate success and thousands of letters and postcards arrived at the Society's headquarters backing their aims. Numerous other television, radio and newspaper interviews followed.

The Society's campaign to rid the world of naked animals continued for six years — and fooled many people. The Society was, however, an invention of New York's principal prankster, Alan Abel.

The Dream of Everlasting Beauty

Sarah Rachel Leverson offered Victorian women what they dreamed of — everlasting beauty. She claimed that her preparations were the key to a perfect appearance. She sold preparations such as Jordan Water brought by racing camel from the River Jordan itself. In actual fact the water she used came direct from her kitchen tap. She also sold magnetic rock which contained the secret of everlasting beauty, dew of the Sahara which got rid of wrinkles, a beauty preparation supposedly made for the Sultana of Turkey and used by Europe's Royal Brides, and many other beauty products. As these cost anything from £200 to £1000, depending upon the buyer's status in society, Sarah became quite rich.

Sarah then turned to blackmailing her clients. But one of them went to the police and Sarah's lucrative career came to an end.

Monster from the Depths

I n 1845, Dr Albert C Koch exhibited the skeleton of a 34.5-metre (114-foot) long sea serpent. Koch charged visitors 25 cents to see his amazing fossil. He did quite well until Professor Jeffries Wyman, an anatomist, decided to examine it. He discovered that the serpent had been made from the bones of several creatures and was a fake.

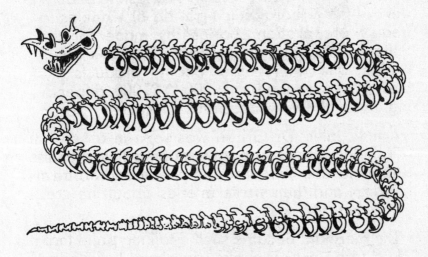

Undeterred, Koch simply changed the name of the creature and exhibited it somewhere else. He was exposed as a hoaxer several times, but each time he simply moved on to another place, making money as he went.

Mermaid Fever

I n the late 1840s, reports appeared in several American newspapers about a stuffed mermaid-like creature. It belonged to Dr Griffin from the Lyceum of Natural History in London and he had brought it from a museum in China.

A little later, Dr Griffin was seen in a hotel in Philadelphia. Newspaper reporters went to the hotel to see the amazing mermaid for themselves, and then wrote articles about the creature they had seen.

The mermaid became such a talking point that it had to be put on public show, and hundreds of people queued to see it. Eventually it was revealed that the mermaid was a fake. Dr Griffin did not exist, and the whole episode had been a hoax devised by master showman, Phineas Taylor Barnum.

Lustig's Money-making Machine

C ount' Victor Lustig, whose main claim to fame was that he sold the Eiffel Tower in 1925, was once imprisoned in Texas, USA. He managed to get out of the jail when he discovered that the sheriff had been fiddling the accounts. Lustig talked him into buying a remarkable money-making machine that could produce $100 bills.

Lustig was released but the sheriff soon realized he had been duped, and once again Lustig was arrested. This time he was released by convincing the gullible sheriff that he had devised a foolproof counterfeiting system and that he needed only $65 000 to perfect it. The sheriff robbed the county funds for the money which was never recovered.

Humbert's Inheritance

When Thérèse Humbert heard groans coming from the next railway compartment she bravely climbed along the outside of the train to see what she could do. In the compartment she found a man who had just had a heart attack. She climbed in and helped him, and the man, Robert Henry Crawford, said he would be eternally grateful to her for saving his life and would reward her one day.

Two years later, in 1881, Thérèse received a letter saying that Crawford had died and made her a beneficiary in his will. The will said that Thérèse was to look after the family fortune, which was locked in a safe, until her younger sister, Marie, was old enough to marry one of Crawford's two nephews.

The story of the inheritance enabled Thérèse and her husband to obtain loans and improve their lifestyle. Eventually, larger loans had to be raised to cover the interest on the original loans. For 20 years, the Humberts were able to live in luxury in spite of attempts to discredit Thérèse's story. But by 1902, financiers realized that the amount of the inheritance would not be enough to cover all the loans and legal costs that had arisen. Calls were made for the safe to be opened. When it was opened, the authorities

found a brick and an English halfpenny, but by this time the Humberts had disappeared. They were arrested in Madrid in December, 1902.

Thérèse was jailed for five years and her two brothers, who had played the fictitious nephews of the non-existent Robert Crawford, were sentenced to two and three years each.

Sooty's Monster Moth

Many parents in Britain telephoned the BBC when it was announced that a monster moth had chewed its way through the original glove puppets of Sooty and Sweep, worth £10 000. Apparently, their children were really distressed to hear that their favourite TV puppets had died in such a way. Eventually, Matthew Corbett, who took over the puppet series from his father Harry, had to admit that the story was just an April Fool hoax.

Just the Job

Golf club steward, Ken Lawrence, and his wife received quite a shock in 1983 when they opened their local paper to find their jobs being advertised. Luckily, they had a sense of humour and as the date was 1 April they realized the advertisement was just a joke. But the joke did not seem quite so funny when they were inundated with applicants for the jobs.

Hovercraft Hoax

On 1 April, 1980, Capital Radio, in London, announced that hovercraft services from Heathrow airport had been cancelled because of the low tide. Heathrow is well inland, so one wonders how many people believed it.

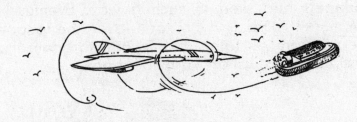

Wrong Flight

A group of businessmen flying to Belfast on 1 April, 1980, were surprised to hear the announcement, 'We shall shortly be arriving in Paris'. Some of them may have hoped it was true — but it turned out to be yet another April Fool hoax.